T0271549

FORGET ABOUT
SUSTAINABILITY
FIRST YOU NEED
AN IDEA

BIS Publishers

DESIGN FOR
SUSTAINABILITY
SURVIVAL
GUIDE

1. YOU'RE IN THE MIDDLE

By now, you must have received a zillion warning messages that human life on earth needs to quickly become more sustainable, or else. No more of that. Each page of this book provides short and well-illustrated opportunities to help you participate in design for sustainability projects.

These themes are currently part of ongoing discussions at design schools, government institutions, and companies. The cluster of challenges seems overwhelming, but there's a shimmer of light at the end of the tunnel. You're lucky, because you're now able to better participate in a pleasurable and rewarding activity: reducing humanity's planetary harm.

This book is not a call for action. You've already started.

Bodystorming

You sleep.
You eat.
You clean.
You sit around.
You move.
You have feelings.
You communicate.
You buy stuff.

You're a consumer. No doubt about it – you're the easiest subject to study close up.

You're the one who experiences your life changes first-hand. Consider your considerations – judge your judgements. Find out what it means to live green and to buy responsibly, even if only for a week.

What does it feel like to refrain from smartphone use, personal purchases, and high-speed travel? Do you feel deprived and sad, or possibly elated and empowered? Or is it simply no big deal?

Keep a personal diary for professional use.

Read and be critical

Text is everywhere, ready for you to absorb and think about critically. Stay informed. Know what's going on in the world, in science and in your profession. You read books, articles, websites, blogs, social media. No matter what you read, be aware where it comes from.

Text is the product of transformations. Scientists always assume things.

Media prefer juicy stories or potential threats to facts. Note how exclamation and question marks are used to try to grab your attention!?

When you look for information, fold away the blanket of the implausible.

1.3 YOU'RE IN THE MIDDLE

Ancestors and peers

The quest for a sustainable world is still young. Philosophers were the first to send out warning signals. Malthus expected huge shortages, Illich demonstrated that cars are slower than bicycles.

Many designers have addressed the potential of design for sustainability. They all want to make the world a better place.

Best known: Viktor Papanek. He didn't often use the word sustainability, but he saw what's coming. Richard Buckminster Fuller, famous for his ideas of reduction said, 'Use less and less to do more and more'. He was a technological progress visionary in the 20th century.

There are many others. Trace them. Find the origins of the principles of reuse, recycling, and efficient energy conversion and storage.

Converse with peers, preferably in informal settings. One idea leads to the next.

Talking never harmed anyone.

IVAN ILLICH

Tools for Conviviality

'The average American puts in 1,600 hours to get 7,500 miles out of his car; that's less than five miles per hour. In countries deprived of a transportation industry, people manage to do the same, walking wherever they want to go...' ('Energy and Equity', Illich, 1974, p.19). Below: Image of the 2021 Victor Papanek exhibition 'The politics of design'

Arrange and store

Keep a list of what you've read and plan to read.
If what you're reading is interesting, make small maps of understanding.

Start your personal file of 'Fascinating Quotes'.

Images enrich examples. Store them in a special place. Don't exclude the bad ones. While 'Right' inspires, 'Wrong' motivates at least as much to find right answers. Pictures stick in your mind. Organize images, cherry pick them. Create different albums; this will help you find your way through those mountains of information.

Curate your collection and share it.

Your collection will be your idea repository, the basement of your way of thinking. In due time it will map your progress of insights. Your archive is your mind's autobiography.

Throughout his life, Richard Buckminster Fuller archived 80 meters of 'Chronofiles', documenting his life every 15 minutes from 1920 to 1983. There's absolutely no obligation to match this.

'Cigar Box Encyclopædia' (2000) by Aldwyth. This piece includes 26 separate collaged cigar boxes, one for each letter of the alphabet (shown are M, B, P and T).

Travel stories

There's a Chinese saying: 'Tell me and I'll forget, teach me and I'll remember, engage me and I'll learn'. The best way to get engaged in sustainability is to go places and talk to people. Memorable stories and unexpected perspectives will emerge.

Examples: A person who works at a waste disposal facility tells you that the amount of waste plummeted when the economy collapsed. In a sustainable fashion store, the shopkeeper says that customers can bring their clothes back to be resold. At a repair café, a volunteer shows you that almost all the coffee makers brought in for repair don't need repair, they simply need descaling.

YouTube is cold. Reality is hot.

Travel, undergo and observe with a critical eye. Visit factories, design studios, landfills, start-ups, wind turbine facilities, shopping malls. Interview pioneers, CEOs, chefs, market traders. And don't overlook the customers.

Oh yes... and don't read all this. Go on a field trip instead.

Ambition

We're not asking you to be hugely ambitious and save the world. On your own you can't remove all the garbage from every beach. It's all about proportion. You certainly should be eager to improve things, but you'd better limit your efforts to your own circle of influence.

Ambition is personal. When taking up a challenge, there's always that inner voice whispering 'as best you can'.

And you're not alone. Commitment gets things done. Always involve others.

- You may not have as much power as you'd wish, but the effect of influence can be just as strong.
- Change takes time. The more urgent the crisis, the quicker the changes.
- Prevent urgency from getting out of hand.

By the way, the word 'ambition' isn't worth googling; brainy quotes about ambition are boring.

TIPS FOR FURTHER READING (in chronological order)

- **Thomas Malthus (1826) AN ESSAY ON THE PRINCIPLE OF POPULATION, or A view of its Past and Present Effects on Human Happiness; with an Inquiry into our Prospects respecting the Future Removal or Mitigation of the Evils which it Occasions.** *John Murray. 6th ed. 2 vols.* Malthus' theory states that population growth will always outrun food supply, requiring limits on human reproduction (or risk famine, war, and disease). His book caused furious controversy.

- **R. Buckminster Fuller (1969) OPERATING MANUAL FOR SPACESHIP EARTH.** *Lars Müller Publishers.* Fuller calls for a design revolution and offers advice on how to guide spaceship Earth toward a sustainable future.

- **Ivan Illich (1974) ENERGY AND EQUITY.** *Calder & Boyars Ltd.* In this essay, philosopher Illich argues for the inversion of industrial progress to allow humans to survive and live decently. After a certain point, he says, more energy gives negative returns. For example, moving around causes loss of time proportional to the amount of energy poured into the transport system, so that the speed of the fastest traveler correlates inversely to the equality as well as freedom of the median traveler.

- **Herman Daly (1977) STEADY STATE ECONOMICS.** *Freeman.* A foundational text on the economics of sustainability. Enough is best.

- **Janine Benyus (1997) BIOMIMICRY; Innovation Inspired by Nature.** *Harper Collins.* Benyus studies nature's most successful ideas and adapts them for human (and sustainable) use.

- **C.K. Prahalad (2004) THE FORTUNE AT THE BOTTOM OF THE PYRAMID; Eradicating Poverty Through Profits.** *Wharton School Publishing.* Caused a revolution in thinking about poverty alleviation, viewing the poorest as source of value creation and wealth. Not without ethical ramifications.

- **Kate Fletcher & Linda Grose (2011) FASHION & SUSTAINABILITY; Design for Change.** *Laurence King Publishing.* One of the first books to address the problems of fast fashion.

- **R. BUCKMINSTER FULLER COLLECTION (Chronofiles).** The Stanford Libraries and the Estate of R. Buckminster Fuller maintain a digital archive with materials relating to his career as an architect, system theorist, designer, and inventor. *https://exhibits.stanford.edu/bucky*

Victor Papanek (1971) DESIGN FOR THE REAL WORLD; Human Ecology and Social Change. *Pantheon Books.* The world's most widely read book on design, advocating the socially and ecologically responsible design of products, tools, and community infrastructures.

A BANTAM BOOK · $2.25 · B7591

Why the Things You Buy Are Expensive, Badly Designed, Unsafe, and Usually Don't Work!

With some startling practical alternatives-- like a radio that costs 9c, a $6 refrigerator, a television set for $8, and much, much more!

Design For The Real World
by Victor Papanek

Human Ecology and Social Change

With an Introduction by R. Buckminster Fuller

Completely Illustrated

2. BENCHMARKS

The only way to effectively approach sustainability is from a systems perspective. You need to consider a wide perspective before diving into details.

There are no ready-made design approaches that guide you through all that is important about sustainability. Instead, you must learn to patch together a series of different approaches, frameworks, and visions in order to build a sustainable solution. These are presented here as benchmarks. Use these to better understand and shape your own sustainable design process.

Some benchmarks clearly indicate what should be done and how to go about it, others are more ambiguous; they'll help you reflect on your norms and values as a designer.

Sustainability is going to become more important as time passes. Work with these benchmarks. Choose the ones you like best and use them to improve your sustainable design skills. It will make you a better designer, if nothing else.

Economic paradise has arrived! Or has it?

This is what growth ultimately and supposedly entails.

Every human is entitled to the following commodities:
- More than sufficient food of any kind.
- A proper family home.
- Fast transportation everywhere, including outer space-climate control both indoors and outside.
- Permanent telecommunication with everyone through all media.
- Every knick-knack and gadget imaginable, available to all.
- Energy for anything.
- Events and entertainment 24/7
- Enjoyable open spaces in woods, fields, and urban areas.
- Clean pools, rivers, and seas for swimming.
- Pleasurable wildlife.
- Limitless choice of apparel.
- Etcetera.

Let's try and get this omnipresent paradise going for everyone, but then sustainably.

Hmm.. tricky.

The UN Sustainable Development Goals

Formulating seventeen goals for better and more sustainable human life on earth that 193 nations agree on in eight months (January – August 2015) is an amazing accomplishment. That year, the assembly adopted 'Transforming our world: the 2030 Agenda for Sustainable Development'. It came with 169 targets and 232 indicators designed to help countries end poverty, protect the planet, and ensure prosperity for all. It's imperative to check whether progress is being made so the framework of outcomes is reviewed regularly.

The Sustainable Development Goals (SDGs) have some overlapping and contradictory goals – an inevitable result of 193 nations sitting together. They are certainly not perfect. But they do provide a common direction for travel. Consider them carefully and critically.

Decoupling

A nation's Gross Domestic Product (GDP) is the total of 'relevant' economic transactions. GDP keeps on growing while resources shrink; the side-effects are soaring. There you go. Economic growth and sustainability seem to be mutually exclusive. What to do?

There's a convenient economic assumption, which states that economies can grow and simultaneously spare the environment.

Decoupling is the word, which comes with many popular labels and guises:

- Win-win scenario: making a profit on sustainable output.
- Factor 4: doubling human wealth with half the consumption of nature.
- Sustainable growth: euphemistic and typical policy jargon.

Decoupling is extremely difficult; it fails most of the time. Economists seem to be unwilling to question the primacy of economic growth. Coupling and revision of economics might help.

Today, commoning refers to initiatives where material or immaterial resources are shared among a community of users who together determine the rules on management and use of their resources. Below: Greek philosopher Diogenes yearned to be free from material worries and the complexities and vanities of social convention. So he stripped down to the simplest life possible and became kynikos (dog-like) or cynical.

Limits to growth

It's 1970. We're just starting to recognize environmental issues. Scientists are publishing articles on pollution and ecological changes. The first environmental activists have given warning signs. Few people care.

The world's wake-up call is 'The Limits to Growth' published by The Club of Rome in 1972. It compiles information from all parts of the world and signals the trends in increasing pollution and resource exhaustion. It states that the Earth's ecosystems will hardly be able to support economic and population growth beyond the year 2100. The public begins to take notice: Homo sapiens could become an endangered species.

The emphasis has since shifted from pollution and food shortages to climate change, wastefulness, shrinking biodiversity, and dependence on cheap labor.

Nevertheless, the 1972 warning was, and is, spot on. Scientists have now been sounding the alarm for decades.
Change is due.

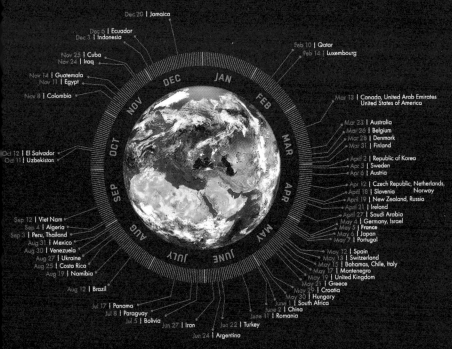

Earth Overshoot Day marks the date when humanity's demand for ecological resources and services in a given year exceeds what our Earth can regenerate in that year. In 2021, it fell on July 29. For the rest of the year, we were operating in overshoot; it would take 1.7 planet Earths to meet human demand.

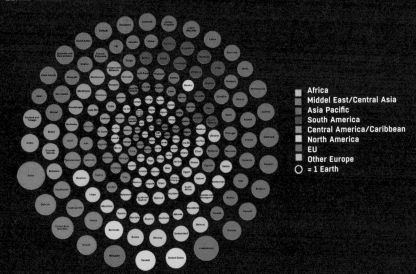

Africa
Middel East/Central Asia
Asia Pacific
South America
Central America/Caribbean
North America
EU
Other Europe
○ = 1 Earth

Abundance

So far, we've made admirable progress. We can feed more people than ever before. Life expectancy is increasing. The number of people is gradually stabilizing. We've learned to get access to plenty of resources through innovation.

We can now make and do things that were unimaginable a few years ago. Technology has made us so invincibly smart – a glorious future lies ahead.

Now we're talking! Established truths make great promises. But the advocates of abundance have overlooked a few things:

- We have put the environment at great risk. And there is no guarantee of wonderful future discoveries. We can't exploit the not yet invented.
- New phenomena may be uncontrollable.
- Believers in abundance use narrow frames to imagine wide horizons.

Lesson 1: The abundance we ache for is not technological. We need an abundance of wellbeing and culture.

Lesson 2: Beware of statements like 'the sun provides energy to supply humanity 10,000 times over'. Sure, with a zillion new devices and miles of infrastructure, let alone the use of other countries' deserts.

Lesson 3: Include all possible side effects of the entire system to understand your idea.

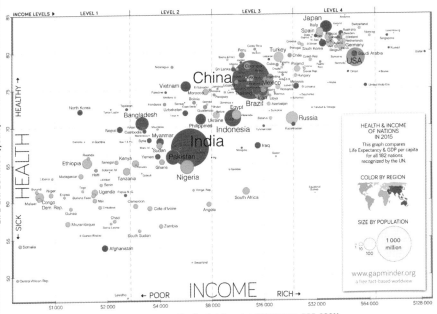

GDP PER CAPITA ($ adjusted for price differences, PPP 2021)

We need to better understand facts and data. Hans Roslin was an expert, he said: 'People often call me an optimist because I show them the enormous progress they didn't know about. That makes me angry. I'm not an optimist. I'm a very serious 'possibilist'. As a possibilist, I see all this progress and it fills me with conviction and hope that further progress is possible. This is not optimistic. It's having a clear and reasonable idea about how things are.'

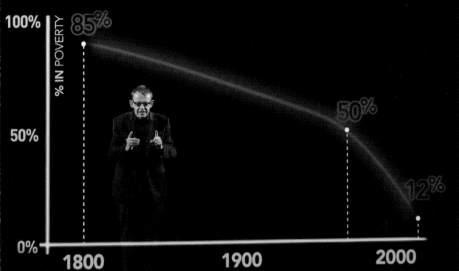

Eco-design

The 1990s saw the emergence of eco-design. Eco-design is about understanding a product's environmental impact across its entire life cycle, from raw materials to end of life.

Companies like this approach because it gives them something to measure.

Now they can compare any product designed under a regime of environmental concerns with its non-eco predecessor.

Most products do not meet all eco-requirements. Products that can be (technically) recycled are often not because of insufficient flow control and those labelled as 'recycled' may only have been through the shredder once. Nevertheless, eco-design can save energy and materials. And, of course, money.

Life Cycle Assessment (LCA) is a tool for assessing and comparing products' sustainability. Another measure is the EU Ecodesign Directive which has resulted in improvements in products' energy efficiency. Although legislation is slow and often 'after the fact', it does produce a bottom line of minimum requirements.

No matter how supportive eco-design is, it leaves moral questions out of the equation. Many products are pointless. Take the least essential product you can possibly imagine. Eco-design it and consequentially wonder if that makes sense.

The nighttime view of Earth illuminates trends in urbanization and energy consumption.

1970s US postage stamp blocks to raise public awareness about the need to protect our planet's ecosystems.

ECO-DESIGN CHECKLIST

The requirements are obvious:
- Reduce materials used
- Use recycled or reclaimed materials
- Use renewable resources
- Minimize manufacturing waste
- Eliminate toxic emissions
- Minimize energy use in production
- Reduce product packaging volume and/or weight
- Use low-impact transport systems
- Design to encourage low-consumption behaviour
- Reduce energy during use
- Design for durability
- Design for reuse and repair
- Design for recycling
- Design for safe disposal
- One word says it all: eco-efficient

Cradle to Cradle

Cradle to cradle became all the rage in 2002 when William McDonough and Michael Braungart published 'Cradle to Cradle; Remaking the Way we make Things'. It appealed to designers. The message was uplifting: waste = food, use solar income, respect diversity.

Many people love the idea of waste being food for upcycling. However, materials' physical properties almost always deteriorate when recycled, making upcycling difficult. Moreover, economic principles stand in the way. Even a closed-loop economy can spiral out of control through excess consumption. Reduction of material flows is absent.

Even more uplifting than Cradle to Cradle was the update 'The Upcycle: Beyond Sustainability – Designing for Abundance'. Up, up, up. The fundamentally good idea is that businesses improve the planet, rather than use its resources efficiently. The authors' view on time is inspiring: a single cycle of product reuse is of no consequence. Sustainability only becomes serious business with an outlook of at least five lives.

Cradle to Cradle, or C2C, carries the aura of abundance. Literally. As always: watch out for sweeping statements. C2C itself is a business.

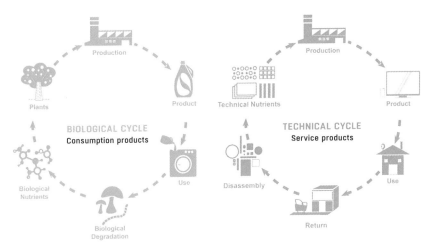

Cradle to Cradle recognizes two cycles for materials: the technical and the biological cycle. The 'waste' materials in an old product become the 'food' for a new product. Below: Viewing Machine by Olafur Eliasson, 2001-2003, Park Inhotim, Brumadinho, Minas Gerais, Brazil. The sculpture works as a tool to modify our vision of the world.

Circularity

Here we have today's number 1 benchmark. It's Circularity! Everybody wants to be circular. Circular looks good on you.

The Ellen MacArthur Foundation introduced its philosophy. The circular economy gives us the tools to tackle climate change and biodiversity loss together, while addressing important social needs.

There is the potential to loop back and slow down the flow of products and materials. Yet a perfect circular economy is as impossible as a perpetuum mobile. There will always be some system leakage. Moreover, circularity doesn't limit consumption.

Take the fast-moving goods: packaging, disposables, fashion. There's always the material flow to organize. Check where it came from and send it where it makes sense. Prevent leakage.

Critical design

Reduction is urgent. There are other words too: degrowth, economic contraction, sufficiency. They needn't be scary. There can be many other kinds of growth. Some scientists dare to propose drastic changes. Economist Tim Jackson touched a nerve with his book 'Prosperity without Growth'. He suggests radical changes in investment intentions, to make them work for the common good rather than for material processing and pointless profits. He proposes a worldwide redesign of economics: what a challenge!

Remember this: the growth of one thing shrinks another. For designers, reduction is a tough deal as they are supposed to come up with new products. Some, though, have chosen an inspiring critical stance. They search for answers.

- Christien Meindertsma analyzed the ashes of burnt waste. She even found gold.
- Riel Bessai designed artificial carbon sinks: a modular system from bio-based plastic units. Each unit sequesters 3 kg of CO_2 from the atmosphere. Products made from these units are to be kept and recycled for hundreds of years.
- Marti Guixé calls himself an ex-designer and masterfully refrains from designing objects.
- Anthony Dunne and Fiona Raby experiment with future projections of upcoming ideas: families producing and selling energy carriers such as hydrogen and blood.

Artificial carbon sinks: a modular system from bio-based plastic units by Riel Bessai.

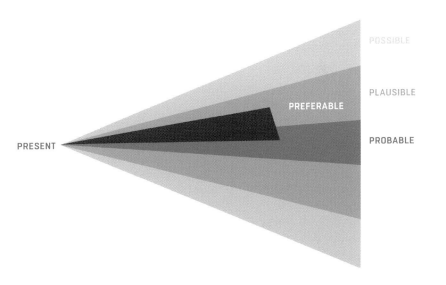

Stuart Candy: The cones fanning out represent different levels of likelihood for potential futures. The probable cone is where most designers operate and how designs are evaluated. Below: Christien Meindertsma, Bottom Ash observatory

Big practices

Apply benchmarks, but importantly, challenge them. Achieving sustainability is not a simple matter of ticking the right boxes.

There's no absolute 'sustainable material' or 'sustainable product'. There are no final answers. Sustainability depends on worldviews, human behavior, and the project at hand.

To develop an overview, we offer crude, often-neglected guidelines. They can help put benchmarks in place, depending on what you're working on.

- Long timelines help define future tasks, so be prepared for decades to come. After the deadline, the lifeline starts.
- Large scale projects are more likely to make a difference.
- A sustainable option merely adds to existing ones. There will be more products and energy consumption than before so we need overruling alternatives to reduce the flows.
- Bearing witness to sustainability improvement is not sufficient; get the evidence.
- It takes more than awareness for people to change their behavior. Learn about social habits: consumers have them, companies have them, design studios have them, you have them. Social psychology provides principles for behavioral change.
- Be wary of data processing devices. They're not harmless.

TIPS FOR FURTHER READING (in chronological order)

- Donella H. Meadows, Jorgen Randers, Dennis L. Meadows (1972) THE LIMITS TO GROWTH: A Report for the Club of Rome's Project on the Predicament of Mankind. *Universe Books.* Our exponential resource consumption will probably lead to a rather sudden and uncontrollable decline in both population and industrial capacity. Much debated book.

- Ernst Von Weizsäcker, Amory Lovins, Hunter Lovins (1998) FACTOR FOUR; Doubling Wealth, Halving Resource Use. A report to the Club of Rome. *Taylor & Hudson.* The book describes the idea of resource productivity: at least four times as much wealth can be extracted from the resources we use.

- William McDonough and Michael Braungart (2002) CRADLE TO CRADLE: Remaking the Way We Make Things. *Rodale Press.* The book presents three principles that have become common knowledge among designers: Everything is a resource for something else (waste = food); use clean and renewable energy; respect diversity.

- Thomas Princen (2005) THE LOGIC OF SUFFICIENCY. *MIT Press.* What if modern society took ecological constraint as a given, not a hindrance but a source of long-term economic security? How would it organize itself, structure its industry, shape its consumption?

- William McDonough and Michael Braungart (2013) THE UPCYCLE: Beyond Sustainability – Designing for Abundance. *North Point Press.* 'You are alive', the authors argue, 'your toaster is not. Technical products don't die and vanish. This is the problem and the opportunity.'

- Peter H. Diamandis (2015) ABUNDANCE. THE FUTURE IS BETTER THAN YOU THINK. *Simon & Schuster.* Diamandis argues that 'humanity is now entering a period of radical transformation in which technology has the potential to significantly raise the basic standards of living for every man, woman and child on the planet.'

- Steffen et al. (2015) PLANETARY BOUNDARIES: Guiding Human Development on a Changing Planet. *Science, vol. 347 (6223).* The authors identify the nine processes that regulate the stability and resilience of the Earth system and define the quantitative boundaries within which humanity can continue to develop and thrive.

- Kate Raworth (2018) DOUGHNUT ECONOMICS; Seven Ways to Think Like a 21st Century Economist. *Random House.* Raworth offers a radical re-envisioning of the system that has brought us to the point of ruin. Economics is broken, and the planet is paying the price.

- Hans Rosling (2019) FACTFULNESS. Ten Reasons We're Wrong About the World – and Why Things Are Better Than You Think. *Hodder & Stoughton.* The message of this book is the need to understand facts and data, and to recognize the common errors in our perception of the world. Some of Rosling's facts are contested, for instance his position that population isn't a problem and future population growth will sort itself out.

Ap Verheggen, SUNGLACIER (since 2010). *SunGlacier is an efficient system for harvesting water from air. It is a configuration of sunlight, air and gravity that can produce potable water from air nearly anywhere on the planet, even in hot and dry deserts. The system began as an art-meets-science project that can change how water resources are perceived and used.*

- **Katherine Trebeck and Jeremy Williams (2019) THE ECONOMICS OF ARRIVAL; Ideas for a Grown-up Economy.** *Policy Press.* The authors explore the possibility of 'Arrival', urging us to move from enlarging the economy to improving it.

- **Helmut Haberl, et al. (2020) A SYSTEMATIC REVIEW OF THE EVIDENCE ON DECOUPLING OF GDP, RESOURCE USE AND GHG EMISSIONS, PART II: synthesizing the insights.** *Environ. Res. Lett. 15 065003.* The authors conclude: 'large rapid absolute reductions of resource use and GHG emissions cannot be achieved through observed decoupling rates, hence decoupling needs to be complemented by sufficiency-oriented strategies and strict enforcement of absolute reduction targets.'

- **Karine van Doorsselaer and Rudy Koopmans (2020) ECODESIGN: a Life Cycle Approach for a Sustainable Future.** *Hanser Publications.* Ecodesign requires life cycle thinking with the environmental impact minimized at all stages of the product cycle, from the extraction of raw materials to end of use.

- **IPCC (2022) CLIMATE CHANGE 2022: Impacts, Adaptation and Vulnerability.** *Contribution of Working Group II to the Sixth Assessment Report of the Intergovernmental Panel.* The report reviews the capacities and limits of the natural world and human societies to adapt to climate change. *https://www.ipcc.ch*

- **THE UNITED NATIONS SUSTAINABLE DEVELOPMENT GOALS:** *https://sdgs. un.org/goals*

3. THE FORCE WE SERVE

The first law of thermo-dynamics states that energy can be converted in form, but it can neither be created nor destroyed. The unit of energy is the Joule, the amount of work needed to move an object over a distance of one meter with a force of one Newton.

Human civilization requires loads of energy to function which it gets from energy resources such as fossil fuels, nuclear fuel, or renewables. The processes of Earth's climate and ecosystem are driven by the radiant energy Earth receives from the Sun and the geothermal energy contained within the earth.

Energy Superheroine

She is our invisible superheroine. She does everything including moving things, keeping us warm or cool, growing our food and cooking it. Our digital telepathy? She's feeds it. For monetary phenomena look backstage: yes! there she is again. There's no light without her. We love her. But before you know it, she'll disappear, leaving dark traces all over the place.

Our energy 'Superheroine' is a monster, look at all the stuff she's claimed. She wants turbines, solar converters, transformers, heat exchangers, gravity exploiters, mechanisms, and materials with built-in skills. We make them, maintain them, replace them, and on occasion, we recycle them.

To move around, our Superheroine requires carrier substances, fluids, gases, solids. We transport her using cables, wires, tubes, sockets, pipes, valves, roads, ships, trains, harbors, trucks, pumps. We put her in containers, tanks, cannisters, capsules, batteries, and more: these all constitute the infrastructure she can't travel without.

All the goods we make, and use, justify her care: everything from earrings to airplanes and from gadgets to flowers and food. Fortunately, our Superheroine provides the power to support her needs.

She really doesn't care about the rest.

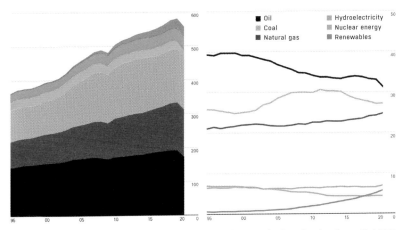

Oil Hydroelectricity
Coal Nuclear energy
Natural gas Renewables

Around **82%** of all energy used in the world comes from coal, oil and natural gas. But **65%** of people wrongly believe that fossil fuels are no longer the dominant energy sources. All the talk about clean energy gives the impression that the old dirty fuels are already being replaced. But nope.

OIL CONSUMPTION 2020
GJ per capita

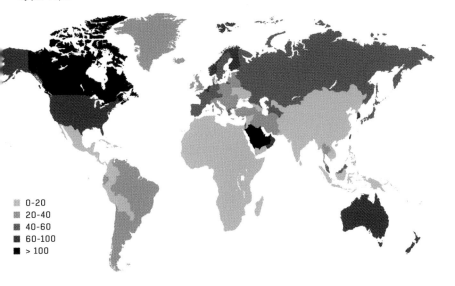

0-20
20-40
40-60
60-100
> 100

The Energy Transition

We know we must go through the Energy Transition to reach the next energy system. It's a lengthy trip – it will take us 30-40 years and it will lead us from burning predominantly fossil fuels to carbon neutrality, or net-zero carbon emissions.

Net-zero carbon means that there is a balance between emissions of carbon dioxide and its removal from the air. This can, for instance, be achieved by removing carbon dioxide through vegetation (planting trees) to make up for emissions elsewhere: offsetting. Doctors would say: we're just fighting the symptoms.

The better option is to use renewable energy and decrease our energy use.

Focus on the transition. Let's make silent electric cars that replace noisy petrol-driven ones. Smell it. Wind farms and solar power replace the power plants that now exploit the heat of burning coal and waste.

Experience the transition. It includes the production, transportation, maintenance, and lifespan extension of batteries, infrastructure, solar panels, and wind turbines.

Currently all this is done with the help of fossil-sourced energy. New energy must overtake the old, to be able to hatch its own life support hardware. The effort is mind boggling. It would help if we stopped using so much energy.

We could start by reminding ourselves what it's all for.

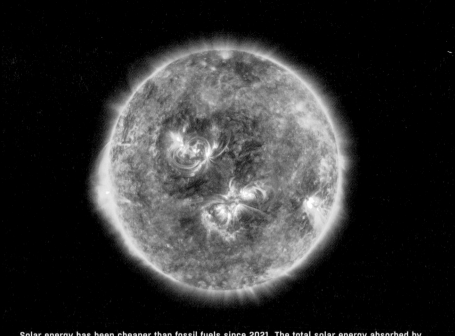

Solar energy has been cheaper than fossil fuels since 2021. The total solar energy absorbed by Earth's atmosphere, oceans and land masses is approximately 3,850,000 exajoules (EJ) per year.

3.3 THE FORCE WE SERVE
Renewable energy

Consider the human timescale. Renewable energy comes from resources that are naturally replenished on a human timescale.

Over millions of years slow accumulation of biomass in the Earth's crust formed oil, coal, and gas. Humanity has burnt roughly half of it, and we're incapable of regenerating this immense power within our lifetime. It is therefore not renewable.

Biomass (mostly plants) currently is the most important – and controversial – source of renewable energy. It supplies 9 percent of the total, with hydropower coming second. Solar photovoltaics (PV), wind, geothermal and tidal together only contribute 2 percent. Fossil fuels and nuclear power deliver by far most of it, totalling 86 percent. Solar PV and wind have been increasing their share exponentially since 2010.

There is a long and steep way to go.

7,000 TWh	
6,000 TWh	Solar
5,000 TWh	Wind
4,000 TWh	
3,000 TWh	
2,000 TWh	Hydropower
1,000 TWh	
0 TWh	

1965   1980   1990   2000   2010

Renewables, including solar, wind, hydro, biofuels, and others, are at the center of the transition to a less carbon-intensive and more sustainable energy system. There's rapid growth in the use of renewables to generate electricity.

Energy Density

Energy occupies space. Imagine you're outside on a sunny day, with your hands outstretched. On your right there's a drop of oil. On your left there's nothing but the warm feeling of sunlight. Now ask a friend to set fire to the oil drop. Ouch!

Feel the difference between left and right. Grasp the concept of energy density, the amount of energy per unit volume. After you've attended to your blistered hand, you learn that the energy density of oil exceeds that of sunlight by about 20 quadrillion times. Because of this, oil is pretty popular. It is what makes it so difficult to start using solar energy instead.

It got physicist David MacKay calculating what a transition towards renewable energy implies. He took the UK as example.

You need a lot of land area to put the dispersed power of sunlight, wind, and water to good use. Energy facilities would just about cover the entire country.

Waves, for instance, could provide a meaningful contribution, provided wave farms covered 500 kilometers of coastline. Energy crops, vegetation solely grown to provide energy, would need to cover 75 percent of the entire country.

All that space!

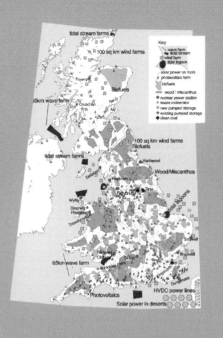

How to replace fossil fuels? In his book 'Sustainable Energy', David MacKay discusses the land area of the UK required to implement each type of sustainable energy. He concludes that at present rates of individual consumption there is no way we can meet our energy needs from renewables without also including nuclear power in the mix and/or completely industrializing the landscape. Below: Areal view of a 30 megawatt solar plant in China's Qinghai province

Zero carbon fuels

Non-fossil fuels, without carbon, and free of CO_2 emissions, are available. Uranium has an extremely high energy density. One fingertip of it equals a barrel of oil. Nuclear energy plants became feasible in the mid 1950s. Sort of feasible. They're very expensive to deploy and quite vulnerable.

Hydrogen is considered a major opportunity for clean energy. Hydrogen's energy density is about a quarter of fossil fuel when stored as a compressed gas. You can burn hydrogen for heat or send it through a fuel cell for current.

The usual illustration of hydrogen is water dripping from the exhaust pipe of a fuel cell driven car. A fuel cell is like a battery, but it cannot be charged. Instead, it generates electricity from the input of hydrogen and oxygen.

Although hydrogen is omnipresent, we cannot harvest it. Other atoms feel attached to it so we have to free it by splitting water or by disengaging it from more complicated molecules. It takes a lot of wind or solar energy to arrive at a gas with the right energy density.

Offshore hydrogen production powerd by wave energy systems. Below: Combined heat and power. Waste heat is stored and used in other industrial processes or for district heating.

Energy elephants

Scale is crucial for the energy transition to make sense. Yes, CO_2 emissions will decrease, but we need products (like solar panels) and infrastructure to make it happen. These are constructed from materials, many of which are valuable and hard to get metals, such as nickel to improve steel alloys, silver for solar cells, and cobalt and lithium for car batteries. A single EV battery could contain 8 kg of lithium, 35 kg of nickel, 20 kg of manganese and 14 kg of cobalt. Mining these metals comes at a cost: CO_2 emissions and pollution.

The challenge is enormous. We're scaling up so rapidly that we're heading towards all kinds of supply and environmental problems. Panels designed for long-term use and recycling are still in their infancy. They're likely to improve and eventually will become better suited for continuous energy production.

Another solution entails radical changes in material composition. You can't change a material without affecting design requirements. In the current setting there are no obvious alternatives, or they would have already been chosen: PV cells may be less efficient without silver; electric cars would be much less efficient without lithium-ion batteries. Different designs with sodium as an alternative are being developed, but the (side)effects are as yet unclear.

Materials required for the energy transition are the elephant in the room.

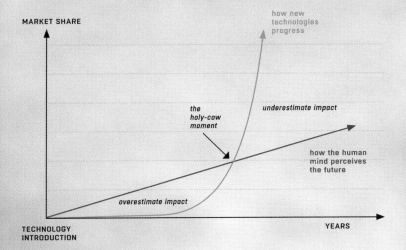

MARKET SHARE

how new
technologies
progress

the
holy-cow
moment

underestimate impact

how the human
mind perceives
the future

overestimate impact

TECHNOLOGY
INTRODUCTION

YEARS

The holy-cow moment is the point when people realize the true meaning of exponential growth: that from that point onwards, change will keep accelerating rather than slow down. (Sprecher & Kleijn, 2019). Below: Manned Cloud designed by Jean-Marie Massaud is a floating hotel. Re-experience travelling, timelessness, and the beauty of the world without being intrusive or exploitative.

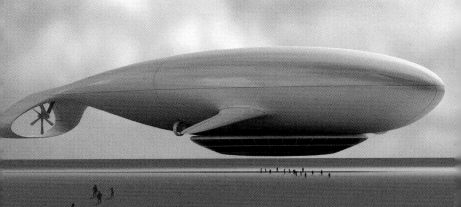

2000 Watt for inspiration

You must feel where this is going. The Transition without decreasing our energy consumption is unlikely to succeed. Many of us know this and propose to include lifestyle changes in the developmental necessities of the Transition.

By the end of the 1990's In Switzerland a vision emerged: the 2000-Watt Society. Three goals were defined:
• Efficiency: use less energy for the same purpose
• Consistency: use renewable energy sources
• Sufficiency: use less for a better quality of life

The ideals are there. Yet the first two goals have the flavour of decoupling: Keep things as they are despite reduction in energy use. Future renewability of energy sources is assumed. But the third goal, sufficiency, defined as 2000 Watt per person is intriguing. Here we are heading for lifestyle changes.

Unmentioned are practical implications, such as lightweight or muscle-powered transportation, the bravado of a cold shower, special rules for non-essential items (as we've seen during Covid), conspicuous idleness, growing vegetables in the windowsill, staying close to home, rationing energy, getting physical, bringing handwritten letters personally, wrapping yourself in a gloriously warm wide onesie, Friday invention day, neighbourhood doorbell dancing mobs (who needs a phone anyway?).

List twenty more examples of a pleasant 2000-Watt life.

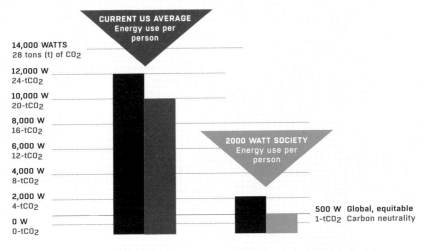

The carbon-neutrality target for all: 1-ton CO_2 per person per year or 500 Watt hours of non-renewable source energy. Below: The '2000 Watt society' is a vision for a future when everyone lives within an energy budget of 2000 Watt hours (primary energy). Three strategies to meet the 2000 Watt hours goals are efficiency, consistency and sufficiency.

Small scale energy harvesting

Ambient low energy phenomena don't mind being converted into energy. Vibrations, magnetism, heat, light, deformation, air pressure, friction, and gravity: all are potential energy converters. They can become sensors and converters in wearable products and smart textiles, non-wovens, and foils. For instance:

- Light (photovoltaic energy, or PV) in flexible inorganic films, printable organic films, dye sensitized solar cells and PV filaments and fibers.
- Deformation (piezoelectricity) in polymers, (nano)composites and nanogenerators.
- Triboelectricity (based on friction between different materials) in films, coatings, fibers, textiles and nanogenerators.
- Thermoelectricity in specific modules in textiles.

The earliest example of energy harvesting, the crystal radio using electromagnetic waves, dates back to 1922. The first kinetic watch was released in 1926. Promises of similar inventions have flourished since, but breakthroughs hardly happened. There are similarities in expectations from nuclear fusion, self-producing nano-robots, and smart refrigerators that organize your shopping. The latter have been in the news for over 40 years.

Energy harvesting could blossom if it wasn't so dependent on irregular input.

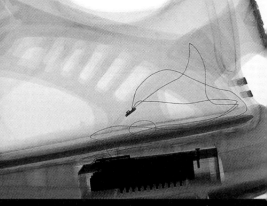

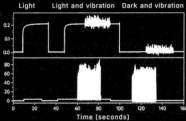

Light | Light and vibration | Dark and vibration

Time (seconds)

Designer Ermi van Oers has created a lamp that uses a living plant to generate its own electricity. German researchers have developed shoes that harvest the energy humans create with every step they take, getting rid of the need for batteries or adapters to power a person's wearable devices. Below: Click beetles store work to amplify power a thousandfold by deforming their external cuticle.

Human powered products

And what about us humans? Can we harvest the energy we produce ourselves? Sure.

It seems like a no-brainer that we should harvest surplus energy from what we do anyway, things like digesting food, or walking. Scientists have attempted to build cool flashing LED shoes powered by kinetic or piezo-electric elements that turn foot activity into electricity. Batteries, however, easily outperform feet.

Most useful are devices that are designed to turn human effort directly into performance. One man flew a pedal driven helicopter for one minute at a height of 3 meters in 2013. The helicopter is half the size of a soccer field and weighs only 55 kilograms. The brief flight was spectacular as a record, but we don't have to go to such extremes for good solutions.

Think bicycles, canoes, hand-driven dynamos. Some rules of thumb:

- Systems that dampen motion generate surplus energy.
- Variation of power requires energy storage in batteries or capacitors.
- Energy storage tends to reduce efficiency.

Batteries and capacitors are convenient, so don't exclusively implement human power to replace batteries. Combinations are possible.

The Cyclus recharger by designer Satoshi Yanagisawa is spring-driven. A simple twist gives 30 minutes of charging power.

The Sail Trike designed by Pixel and Timber: a human x wind powered hybrid vehicle that uses simple mechanical systems and lightweight design to make transportation safe, sustainable, healthy, and affordable.

Solar EROI estimation

For energy harvesting, solar works best. Solar cars, now appearing, could in the future harvest energy for home applications. The number of products with built-in photovoltaic (PV) cells is on the increase. Some of them work. Every solar-powered calculator, lamp, clock, and fountain pump must make sense.

The first requirement is sufficient Energy Return on Investment, or EROI; that's the ratio between the energy delivered and the energy demanded.

You can calculate EROI for a given solar product (take your pick and try) by making an energy balance table listing input and output contributors. Calculate EROI = Energy Input/Energy Output.

Deal with the outcome: If EROI is smaller than 1: forget it or adjust the product. If EROI is bigger than 1, you're home free, but if EROI is much bigger than 1 then modify it, for instance by PV surface reduction.

The second requirement is importance. Consider if your product is sufficiently essential to deserve energy. If not, it should be interred in the Solar House of Horror.

ENERGY YIELD (E_{IN}) PER DAY/WEEK

Irradiation (G)			W/m²
PV cell surface A	x		m²
PV cell efficiency • if G > 200 W/m², use 10% as a first estimate • if G is < 200 W/m², use 5% as a first estimate	x		
Time of exposure to light	x		h
Energy yield	=		

ENERGY DEMAND (E_{OUT}) PER DAY/WEEK

	P [W] x t [h] =	E [Wh]	
Function 1			Wh
Function 2	+		Wh
Function 3	+		Wh
...	+		Wh
Total energy demand	=		Wh
Ratio E_{in} / E_{out}	E_{in} / E_{out} =		
If E_{in} / E_{out} > 10	Feasible, PV system is over dimensioned, optimize the system		
If 1 < E_{in} / E_{out} < 10	Feasible		
If 0,1 < E_{in} / E_{out} < 1	Try to adjust parameters to make it feasible		
If E_{in} / E_{out} < 0,1	Not feasible		

Product efficiency

Refrigerators eat energy continuously. Vacuum cleaners, dishwashers and other household machinery are regulars. In each case the environmental burden of (mostly) non-renewable energy consumption is considerable.

Maximum energy efficiency depends on user behavior; behavior depends on user awareness:
- Provide feedback on energy consumption with light, sound, and displays.
- Let products automatically switch to low energy modes, but leave it to users when this happens.

Behavior mostly depends on user habits:
- Create energy-efficient default settings.
- Stimulate efficient use: a dishwasher needs to be full, or it won't start.

Cooperate with engineers for optimization:
- Abide by the rules for power consumption in standby modes.
- Make sure energy consumption does not deteriorate after updates.
- Ensure that unneeded components in complex products are shut down when not needed.

Dear readers, let me introduce you to the greatest enemy of energy savings: the rebound effect! Which is us. We spend money saved by energy use reduction on more convenience and capacity. We celebrate the energy efficiency of LED televisions, only to demand bigger screens and higher resolutions. We grudgingly accept energy saving lightbulbs, and then use them to light up our dark gardens.

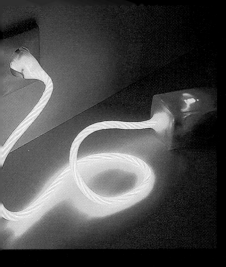

Standby

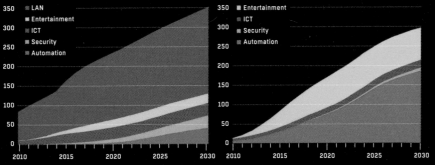

Network active energy consumption and network standby energy consumption

Fighting energy vampires: products that keep consuming energy in standby mode are visible with the power aware cord. Below: The rebound effect: energy efficiency empowerment that generates extra service demand.

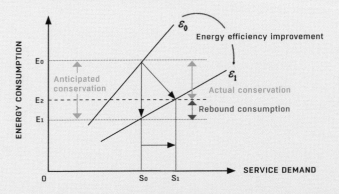

Collective (in)efficiency

Products are individuals within huge populations.
Efficiency multiplies but so does inefficiency. Product weight is usually overlooked as an inefficiency contributor.

Weight awareness has best been developed in air travel. 'Pee before flying' was a policy (briefly). A car is easily 15 times as heavy as its driver. In a region with a million cars on the road each day, the costs of idle weight shifting are grotesque. PET beer kegs are almost 10 times lighter than steel ones and save energy for transportation and recycling.

By and large, the energy efficiency of products is increasing. Individually, smartphones are doing OK, but there's billions of them. Together they consume loads because software and its development demand it. Batteries get drained quickly because of user behavior, which in turn is influenced by the biggest influencers of all: social media providers.

Mining also takes energy. Research suggests that 100 grams of a phone's required elements require 34 kilograms of rock to be processed. Phones are a part of the digital system, which is increasingly energy intensive.

Blockchain distributes calculations, gaining popularity for hiding transactions in crypto currencies, which require massive energy intensive data center capacity.

TIPS FOR FURTHER READING (in chronological order)

- **David MacKay (2009) SUSTAINABILITY - WITHOUT THE HOT AIR.** *Cambridge.* Great book for arithmetic lovers. MacKay asks: how can we power a modern lifestyle without fossil fuels? His answer is sobering: 'Even if we imagine strong efficiency measures and smart technology switches, halving our energy consumption from 125 kWh per day per person to 60 kWh per day, we should not kid ourselves about the scale of the energy challenge which would remain. It would require wind farms with an area equal to Wales and a hundred more nuclear power stations.' www.withouthotair.com

- **K. Ylli et al. (2015) ENERGY HARVESTING FROM HUMAN MOTION: exploiting swing and shock excitations.** *Smart Materials and Structures, 24.*

- **Benjamin Sprecher and René Kleijn (2021) TACKLING MATERIAL CONSTRAINTS ON THE EXPONENTIAL GROWTH OF THE ENERGY TRANSITION.** *One Earth 4.* Very clear description of exponential growth and how it can surprise us (the holy cow moment).

- **International Energy Agency (2022) THE ROLE OF CRITICAL MINERALS IN CLEAN ENERGY TRANSITIONS.** *World Energy Outlook Special Report, IEA.* From the report: 'Our bottom-up assessment suggests that a concerted effort to reach the goals of the Paris Agreement (climate stabilization at well below 2°C global temperature rise) would mean a quadrupling of mineral requirements for clean energy technologies by 2040. The prospect of a rapid increase in demand for critical minerals – well above anything seen previously in most cases – raises huge questions about the availability and reliability of supply.'

- **THE 2000 WATT SOCIETY** is a vision for future where everyone lives within an energy budget of 2000 Watt (primary energy). Three strategies to meet the 2000 Watt goals are Efficiency, Consistency and Sufficiency. www.2000watt.swiss

- **ASKNATURE.ORG.** Online database with many examples of how the living world has evolved to solve intricate problems 'naturally'. Designers interested in biomimicry will find this an invaluable resource.

Olafur Eliassons and Frederik Ottesen, LITTLE SUN (2012). *Little Sun is a work of art and a solar-powered LED lamp that was designed for the 1.2 billion people worldwide living without electricity. There's an alarming statistic that an evening of breathing in the emissions from a kerosene lamp is similar to smoking two packs of cigarettes, not to mention the CO_2 emissions of millions of these lamps. As a social business, Little Sun sustainably handles distribution that benefits off-grid communities, creates local jobs, and generates local profits. Little Sun works with off-grid entrepreneurs to build their own small businesses selling Little Sun lamps, providing them with business starter kits and micro-entrepreneurial training.*

4. USEFULNESS

As soon as users lay their hands on products, the struggle for sustainability starts. They're the ones that can make a difference, provided they get support from designers.

Becoming a savvy customer is really difficult; most of us have a sales victim background. Change requires a revision of nothing less than the assumptions behind growth.

The next step is to help users develop responsible behavior. The means for this are amply available. Applying them must become common sense.

How much is too much?

When you buy something new, it can shame your existing possessions and cause you to replace them.

Today's consumption is all about: confirmation of self-image; optimizing convenience; experiencing magic; function; greed; the feeling of 'a good deal'.

How much and what do we consume in the wealthy parts of the world? Why? Are we happier because of it? How much is enough? How much is too much?

Answering these questions is difficult because it questions the 'good life'. Answering also seems hypocritical, since these questions come from those who consume the most.

Consumption has become part of our economic system to such an extent that it's untouchable. If supplies are tight, we produce more instead of consuming less. Goods are good and more goods are better - that's us. We know what obesity does to us, including the metaphor.

Why's it so hard to talk about consumption without falling in the 'more-is-better' trap?

Clearly, there's a deeper political meaning here. It's easier to keep expanding production and spreading wealth throughout the population than trying to reduce. Economic growth is the lubricant of our consumption society, and vice versa. Economists are wary of challenging assumptions behind 'growth'.

Today humanity uses the equivalent of 1.75 Earths to provide the resources we use and absorb our waste, based on the 2022 edition of the National Footprint and Biocapacity Accounts.

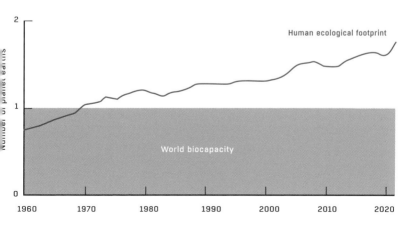

Influencing consumers

Influencing consumers to buy more is well-established professional territory; consumer choices are not isolated acts of rational decision making. Much consumption happens almost sub-consciously. This knowledge is applied in merchandizing and online selling.

Tons of books have been written on ways to control consumer choice, from the best way to display cans of soup to click-baits, and from home delivery (convenience!) to handing out rewards and discounts. We can use this knowledge to stimulate more sustainable consumption.

Energy labels on white goods work surprisingly well to stimulate a more sustainable choice. In Europe, the market share of more efficient appliances increased by 15-38 percent in a decade. Access to organic produce through supermarkets has doubled their consumption. Investment in high-speed trains has led to more people taking the train instead of the plane for short hauls.

We can improve access to more sustainable products, label them transparently, and sell them using sophisticated nudges.

But the thing is, we're still consuming – not reducing. We're merely adding sustainable options as if it's a choice.

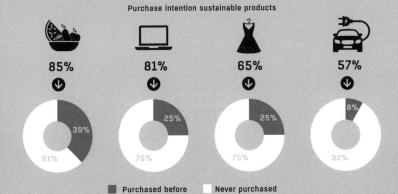

Purchase intention sustainable products

| 85% | 81% | 65% | 57% |

39% Purchased before / 61% Never purchased
25% / 75%
25% / 75%
8% / 92%

■ Purchased before □ Never purchased

Consumers say they intend to buy sustainable products but don't actually buy them. People want everything to be as fast and as cheap as possible. So for traveling long distance, the airplane is the automatic choice. High-speed rail is often faster than flying once you factor in the whole air travel song-and-dance.

Unconsumers

The most sustainable consumption is no consumption.

Government interventions can sometimes work: banning the sales of inefficient incandescent lightbulbs, wasteful single-use plastic bags, and drinking straws. This is choice architecture. The consequence is a massive growth of other kinds of lightbulbs, bags, and straws.

Bottom-up interventions can also work: consumers voluntarily embracing downshifting, slow food, decluttering, and simple living. But you must be able to afford a 'simple' life. Simple living is prone to commercialization; it requires how-to manuals, Marie Kondo workshops, tiny houses, and new slow cookers.

Producer interventions are another way. Fairtrade and other agreements create transparency, waste reduction, and better conditions throughout the value chain. But producers always have a bottom line, and if Fairtrade didn't sell, it wouldn't be there.

Truly sustainable consumption requires a radical transition. Our economic model needs fixing. We need to change the social logic of consumption. In his book 'Prosperity without growth', Tim Jackson provides a long list of recommendations. Designers can contribute by developing and offering viable alternatives to the culture of consumerism.

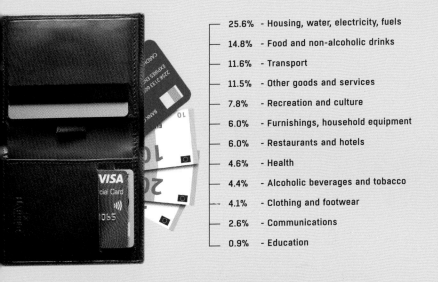

25.6%	- Housing, water, electricity, fuels
14.8%	- Food and non-alcoholic drinks
11.6%	- Transport
11.5%	- Other goods and services
7.8%	- Recreation and culture
6.0%	- Furnishings, household equipment
6.0%	- Restaurants and hotels
4.6%	- Health
4.4%	- Alcoholic beverages and tobacco
4.1%	- Clothing and footwear
2.6%	- Communications
0.9%	- Education

Household expenditure by consumption in the EU in 2022: what would happen if you bought nothing new for a year?

Careful users

The idea of consumption needs drastic rethinking. One possible area for exploration is a shift from consumption to use. Use takes more time; use is about care and careful use contributes to sustainability.

The User is a fictional character in real life. The User drifts around in the minds of designers. The User consists of estimations, assumptions, designer empathy, and a whiff of wishful thinking. Users have more to them then we give them credit for.

Users lead many different lives. A given user often starts as a passive consumer. Then, the active user wakes up. Finally, users become people in disposal dilemmas. They think: 'I no longer use this. Now what?'

We're involved in a cyclical process in which buying, use and discarding have a bearing on design, and where design in its turn influences buying, use and discarding.

We can try to intervene in the cycle to ensure that we activate users and make them care. Design can thus elicit sustainable use.

Design classics by Dieter Rams invite the idea 'to be handled with care'. They'll never look outdated, still function well, and turn out to be valuable. Below: Lay-rationalism: In today's rapid cycles of product innovation, we're often faced with the opportunity to purchase an enhanced product, even though the product we currently own is still fully functional. So, we use our phone in the rain without being aware that our carelessness has an underlying motivation.

Behaviour change agents

The shampoo bottle says: 'Apply on wet hair and leave for 5 minutes'. Effect: an increase in shower water and energy use.

Design is a user behavior influencer. This isn't straightforward as most behavior is subconscious.

Awareness of actions depends on the kind of choices to be made. You may grab a pencil without thinking, but you consciously consider the dilemma. Red or blue?

Consciousness emerges when intuition fails. Conscious motivation can educate intuition, possibly leading to new habits.

Five strategies can change user behavior. They're arranged according to strictness:

Informing: provide clear and relevant information to the conscious mind. 'Please take care of your dotdotdot'.

Feedback: directly or indirectly, the system signals right or wrong. Your dotdotdot says 'beep', blinks, and/or provides meaningful information.

Encouraging: nudging by seduction and rewards. Your dotdotdot tempts you to be sustainable unwittingly.

Steering: enforcing behavioural change. Your dotdotdot use is embedded in regulations with sanctions.

Forcing: undesired behaviour is no option. Your dotdotdot system cannot be used unsustainably

USER	POWER IN DECISION MAKING	
ECO-FEEDBACK	Provides visual, auditive or tactile signs as reminders to inform users of resource use.	GUIDES CHANGE
BEHAVIOUR STEERING	Encourages users to behave in ways prescribed by the designer through the embedded affordances and constraints.	MAINTAINS CHANGE
PERSUASIVE TECHNOLOGY	Employs persuasive methods to change what people think or do, sometimes without their knowledge or consent.	ENSURES CHANGE

PRODUCT

FIT FOR WORK

Never work or drive under the effects of drugs or alcohol

SAFETY FIRST

DOORS & DESK DRAWERS

Keep doors and drawers closed when not in use

SAFETY FIRST

EMERGENCY PROCEDURES

Know your site emergency procedures

SAFETY FIRST

HOT LIQUIDS & SURFACES

Avoid burns and scalds from hot liquids and surfaces

SAFETY FIRST

STAIRS

Avoid falling, use hand rail

SAFETY FIRST

ACCESSING HIGH SHELVES

Use a safe method when accessing high shelves

SAFETY FIRST

4.6 USEFULNESS

Persuasive messaging

Information formats must respond to human peculiarities. A master of persuasive messaging is Robert Cialdini, who found out that the persuasive power of 'be like us' is considerable.

According to Cialdini, the following is true:

- Not everyone always makes a sensible choice based on the available information.
- People use shortcuts.
- Shortcuts can be affected.

Take the hotel bathroom towel message: guests are uninterested in 'Help save the environment- reuse the towels'.

The message, 'Most people who stayed in this room reused their towels at least once during their stay' turns out to be 33 percent more effective in saving laundry costs.

Cialdini's weapons of influence

4.7 USEFULNESS
Readable performance

BEEEP. What on earth is that? After 10 minutes wandering through the house the source is identified. The freezer door is ajar.

Feedback communicates the results of interaction, making it both perceivable and understandable. It helps the user keep track of performance.

Feedback on energy consumption can be a great behavior educator. Smart thermostats prove this, some can tell you precisely how many kWh you used in the past weeks or months. Unfortunately, many people don't really know what that means.

You can also compare your performance with your neighbor, which is a more effective strategy. Some thermostats keep you on track by sending reminders to your smartphone. They're not unlike fitness apps.

With feedback, there's a timing issue. Time-lagged feedback may not be noticed and infrequent feedback is difficult to appreciate. This is true except when cycling on an e-bike. Here 'eco' implies extra effort but provides a 'near heroic' experience.

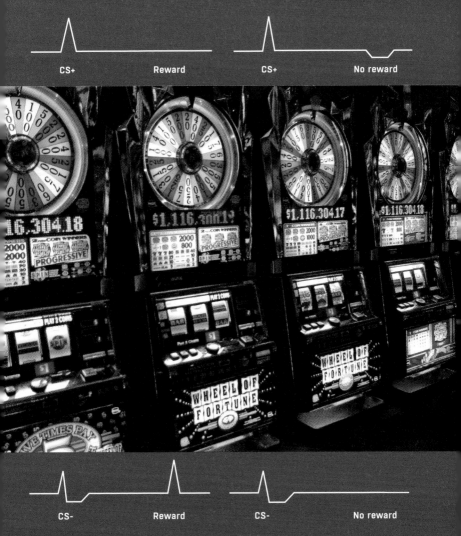

CS+ Reward CS+ No reward

CS- Reward CS- No reward

Players of jackpot or roulette were observed experiencing heightened arousal from the sensory stimulus coming from the machines, regardless of winning or losing. Presentation of an explicit reward-predicting stimulus leads to activation after the stimulus, no response to the predicted reward, and depression when a predicted reward fails to occur. (CS = conditioned stimuli).

Nudging rules instinct

Once upon a time, there was a fairy tale theme park with many attractive rides. Yet it was best known for its garbage gobblers near the spots where you could get refreshments. They were larger than life statues of Big Fat Gus, known for his gargantuan appetite. Their job was to collect snack packaging. Each one kept on asking for more: 'Paper here!' His big mouth had a vacuuming engine. Whenever a visitor held waste in front of him, Big Fat Gus would suck it in and thank the generous giver. Children loved and fed him and unwittingly kept the park tidy forever. Deposits on packaging have the same effect, but without the charm.

Nudging people to behave in a certain way is fascinating. Floor graphics with lines or footsteps can encourage us to use stairs over the escalator. A 2D playing child picture on the street reduces driving speed. A urinal with a decoy fly pictured near the drain directs the urine stream and keeps the toilet clean.

Cues rule instinct: following cues can be rewarding. Subway stairs were designed to make sounds like piano keys. Everyone prefers music and dance over a boring escalator ride.

The Big Fat Gus waste eater that says 'Paper here' and 'Thank You' after feeding him with waste. The French anthropologist, Claude Lévi-Strauss argued that symbol systems and rituals are not reflections of social structure but are imposed on social relations to organize them.

Covert cues

Smaller plates make people eat less in self-service restaurants. Food waste is reduced by some 22 percent. Products like these are more enforcing than friendly encouragement.

Do we want the manipulated to know they are being had?

Think placebo-effect when patients get fake medicine and get cured. There are strong indications that for 'self-observed' inflictions placebos work very well, even when patients know they were given a make-belief treatment. Knowledge of covert cues does not necessarily reduce their effectiveness.

Production of one-way arrow stickers has soared due to Covid requirements. They are simple and convenient. People follow them.

They are very close to rules and regulations, the strictest kind of steering measures. Break those and you know you can be fined or put in prison.

4.10 USEFULNESS
Enforcing behaviour

It is of course possible to enforce 'correct' behavior by supporting regulations with physical means. A valid ticket is essential to open entrance gates to public transportation. Without a coin you can't get a shopping trolley. Some cars won't run unless seatbelts are fastened. You pay extra for overweight luggage in air travel.

Energy input and waste output are the most controllable flows to enforce behavior and remove human intervention from the equation.

Automatic smart thermostats regulate your home's optimal temperature. Insulating buildings is on the way to becoming obligatory, as are built-in speed regulators in cars.

Designers need to consider whether they can stop including inefficient options in the product or service.

There are natural limits to everything, until technology gets involved and people are invited to start going beyond the limits. That is, unless something starts pushing back. Below: Our desire for speed can be tempered with smart built-in speed limitation technology.

IMPACT SPEED kmh		DEATH risk	SERIOUS INJURY risk	SLIGHT INJURY risk
30		10%	15%	75%
40		32%	26%	42%
50		80%	3%	17%
60		95%	3%	2%

Social complexity

Using design to influence human behavior for the better may seem radical, but it's not. Strategies like feedback, encouraging, and steering are a great start. But they don't go far enough as they only focus on individual users and single products. Other options exist, one of these being Practice-Oriented Product Design.

If our goal is sustainable everyday living, we must consider groups of people living their lives, together, with the many things they use. We should attend to the relationships between all these products, and not separately.

If your household decides to change from a gas hob to an induction cooker, it may seem a great sustainable choice as induction cookers are more efficient. But you may also need to rewire the house, remodel the kitchen, and buy a new set of pans. Your cooking schedule may change, as you can now heat up food much faster. This affects your family dinner routine. And so on.

Will the lifestyle in this case be more sustainable? You tell me. And this is just for one family.

Practice-oriented product design asks you to look at life in all its social complexity. Over an extended period.

Brazilian football fans are fans from cradle to grave and now beyond. Sport Club Recife released a special card among their fans to increase organ donations.

MORE COMPLEX

STRATEGIC THINKING
Low difficulty/High complexity

EXPERTISE
High difficulty/High complexity

EASY ← → **HARD**

FLUENCY
Low difficulty/Low complexity

STAMINA
High difficulty/Low complexity

LESS COMPLEX

Consumer scapegoatism

Lifestyles are robust. Developing sustainable habits is almost undoable. We are all tied to an intricate infrastructure that we depend on. It determines our transport, it provides us with water, energy, and food and it helps us to get rid of our garbage and sewage.

We're 'locked-in'.

Breaking free of these bonds is an almost superhuman endeavor. Just try and build your own autarkic house. You'll see.

Governments and others may tell us that we need to limit consumption. They may try to convince us to properly take care of waste. Designers can create smart appliances, LED-lighting, amazing e-bikes, and water-saving showerheads. Nevertheless: electricity sockets tempt us everywhere. Generous showers love to rinse us. Many cities are designed for motorized traffic, not for walking and cycling.

If policies and designers do not address the infrastructures that keep us locked-in into unsustainable behavior, we are turning consumers into scapegoats. We cannot expect consumers to be the main drivers of sustainability. The issue is simply too complex to leave to individual decisions. Keep this in mind in your next sustainable design project.

Target the most influential stakeholder, not the most visible one.

END CLUTTER
Keep products for at least **seven years**

TRAVEL FRESH
If you can, **no personal vehicles**

EAT GREEN
A **plant based diet** — no waste, healthy amount

DRESS RETRO
Three new items of clothing per year

HOLIDAY LOCAL
One flight every three years

CHANGE THE SYSTEM
At least **one life shift** to nudge the system

Science shows that in wealthy countries everyone needs to make these 6 shifts within 10 years (takethejump.org). Below: Mount Recyclemore by British artists Joe Rush and Alex Wreckage portrays the world leaders who attended the G7 Summit in June 2021.

Beyond the familiar

Designers from different regions bring knowledge and experience from their varied backgrounds. Africa can contribute to low energy logistics in the UK. European software can support product life optimization elsewhere.

India understands a thing or two about services.

People's lifestyles are shaped by the culture they're part of. It determines what is considered good or bad, beautiful or ugly. Designers need to be aware of this.

Work on your cultural literacy. Spend time in a different culture.

Observe. Interact. Research. Reflect on another culture's social habits, economic circumstances, local traditions and available technologies.

- Designers also produce culture.
- Assumptions can be harmful.
- Experimentation and cooperation are likely to be productive.

Dabbawalas constitute a smart and efficient lunchbox delivery and return system using bicycles and public transport. Lunch boxes are marked and colour coded with abbreviations for collection points, starting station, handling and destination. Below: In his landmark publication 'Design for the Real World: Human Ecology and Social Change' (1970), Papanek favoured people over profit, demonstrating how design can bring about meaningful social change.

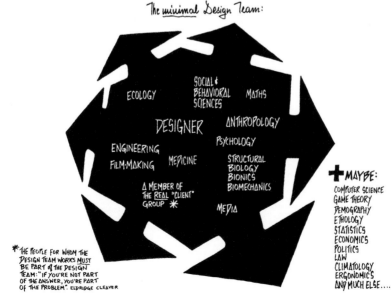

The _minimal_ Design Team:

ECOLOGY

SOCIAL & BEHAVIORAL SCIENCES

MATHS

DESIGNER

ANTHROPOLOGY

PSYCHOLOGY

ENGINEERING

FILM·MAKING

MEDICINE

STRUCTURAL BIOLOGY
BIONICS
BIOMECHANICS

A MEMBER OF THE REAL "CLIENT" GROUP *

MEDIA

+ MAYBE:

COMPUTER SCIENCE
GAME THEORY
DEMOGRAPHY
ETHOLOGY
STATISTICS
ECONOMICS
POLITICS
LAW
CLIMATOLOGY
ERGONOMICS
AND MUCH ELSE....

* THE PEOPLE FOR WHOM THE DESIGN TEAM WORKS MUST BE PART OF THE DESIGN TEAM: "IF YOU'RE NOT PART OF THE ANSWER, YOU'RE PART OF THE PROBLEM". ELDRIDGE CLEAVER

TIPS FOR FURTHER READING (in chronological order)

- **Juliet Schor (1998) THE OVERSPENT AMERICAN: Upscaling, Downshifting, and the New Consumer.** *Basic Books.* How and why can the purchases of others in our social and professional communities put pressure on us to spend more than we can afford to.

- **Thomas Princen, Michael Maniates, Ken Conca (2002) CONFRONTING CONSUMPTION.** *MIT Press.* Tinkering at the margins of production and purchasing will not put society on an ecologically and socially sustainable path. The book explores 'the consumption problem' and documents efforts to confront it.

- **Elisabeth Shove, Matthew Watson, Martin Hand, Jack Ingram (2007) THE DESIGN OF EVERYDAY LIFE.** *Berg Publishers.* Investigating the design, production and use of mass-market goods, the authors offer new interpretations of how consumers' needs are met and manufactured.

- **Debra Lilley (2009) DESIGN FOR SUSTAINABLE BEHAVIOUR: Strategies and Perceptions.** *Design Studies Vol. 30 Issue 6 Pages 704-720.* How could design be used to influence user behaviour towards more sustainable practices?

- **Lewis Akenji (2014) CONSUMER SCAPEGOATISM AND LIMITS TO GREEN CONSUMERISM.** *Journal of Cleaner Production Vol. 63 Pages 13-23.* This paper argues that the consumer is not the most salient agent in the production-consumption system; expecting green consumerism to shift society towards sustainable patterns is consumer scapegoatism.

- **Tim Jackson (2016) PROSPERITY WITHOUT GROWTH; Economics for a Finite Planet.** *Taylor & Francis (2nd ed).* The book summarizes the evidence showing that, beyond a certain point, economic growth does not increase human well-being.

- **Ruben Pater (2018) THE POLITICS OF DESIGN; A (Not So) Global Manual for Visual Communication.** *BIS Publishers.* With communication comes responsibility; are designers aware of the meaning and impact of their work? This book enhances your visual literacy for communication beyond borders and cultures.

- **Robert B. Cialdini (2021) INFLUENCE: THE PSYCHOLOGY OF PERSUASION** *(revised edition). Harper Business Publishers.* Explains the psychology of why people say yes (including 7 principles of persuasion).

- **Dan Lockton, DESIGN WITH INTENT TOOLKIT:** *designwithintent.co.uk* Visual toolkit that aims to give practitioners a more nuanced and critical approach to design and behaviour.

Matthieu Laurette, THE FREEBIE KING (2001). *Hyperrealistic life size sculpture (wax, fiber glass, latex, resin, natural hairs, clothes, shoes, oil painting, CADDIE™ supermarket trolley filled with 100 % money-back products) Laurette's 'Money-back Products' (1993–2001) was his method of shopping and being fully refunded based on the basic marketing system of the major food and commodities corporations. He fed and cleaned himself by almost only ever buying products with 'Satisfied or your money back' or 'Money back on first purchase' offers.*

5. TIME

Implicit use of the notion of time is standard procedure. Time deserves more and better. It's about the length of time products and services are taken care of; the time they're expected to last, as well as what happens afterwards. Things are used for a certain time, which is part of the time they exist.

Nibble on time for a while and taste where it takes you.

Beyond the deadline

Seriously: humans are not very good at dealing with time. Estimation fails, things take longer than foreseen. Perceptions shift and time shrinks. Humans can be tricked into believing they can save time. Planning involves borrowing time from the future through self-imposed urgency.

You all know deadlines. But many of you aren't fully aware that products and services don't really come alive until after you think you're done with them.
It's feedback time! Focusing on the solution, you've created an array of problems. After users start using your creation, only then do they reveal their true behavior. The pointer of the *attention-o-meter* for the result of your work drops.

Ouch! That's only the first scratch. Some users simply forget they own your design. Imperfections make themselves known. Sooner or later, it becomes boring and ugly. Users start longing for improvement, or replacement, or look for an excuse to buy something new.

Now what? It may need repair, an upgrade maybe, or refurbishing. Or it can become an antique and spend decades in the attic. Or, toss it in one of the optional bins: recycling, glass, plastic, household waste. These procedures were hardly addressed prior to the deadline, however, after the deadline is also part of the deal.

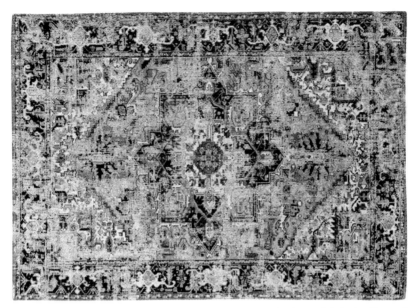

While some once discarded vintage products manage to revive beyond their deadlines other brandnew vintage products start their life beyond the deadline. According to the advertisers 'the artsy patterns of aging create a very dynamic effect and testify to a modern lifestyle.'

5.2 TIME
Products that last

Horror fact: 80 percent of 'broken' coffeemakers are perfectly fine after descaling. The keyword here is care. Care is about proper maintenance: keeping products clean and in working order.

Design must allow for maintenance and show its obviousness. Access to and affordability of repair are design requirements. Support enduring relevance by providing updates. Old is cool; products getting outdated is so 1990.

Care takes time. It clashes with acquired convenience and the habits associated with continuous availability of the new.

Products that last provide a rehab treatment, an antidote against throwaway culture. They elicit care while in use. They're looked after when use time is over. Their afterlife is dignified.

Broken products are returned to their manufacturer, or to new users or intermediates, or they're responsibly disposed of. In any case we created them, and no transformation will make them disappear. They reappear refurbished, or second hand, or divided up in bits and parts. Or they become modern material mines.

Care goes on.

Mechanical watches are designed to last a lifetime, and if taken care of they can last multiple lifetimes. Oil, dirt and dust are often the reason an old watch refuses to run or keeps poor time. They should be serviced every 3-5 years.

Business with care

Carelessness was all the rage in times of economic growth: sell more sell faster. Ignore the costs that carry no price tag. Some companies unconventionally cherish a reputation of selling long-lasting high-value products with top level serviceability. Not everyone can afford them.

We can, though, use services to create more caring business models. 'Servitization' is the word for providing services around products. There are four options to cultivate value and (potentially) improve sustainability:

1. Company takes or buys back the product after use or gives a discount on return. In theory this can be a guarantee that it will be refurbished or otherwise taken care of. Commercial advantage: bond with the customer and possibly sell the same thing more than once.

2. Company owns the product; customers don't. These are product-as-a-service models, or PaaS. Service is the deal and the product is part of it. The company is responsible for the product over time. Its popularity is on the increase as fees are affordable. It has a commercial advantage: the longer it lasts, the more income.

3. Company sells the result of a service: cobbler, dry cleaning service, taxi, or translator, to name a few. Companies that offer a more sustainable service may have a competitive edge.

4. Company brokers use. The business mediates between those who offer and those who need. It is about acquiring, providing, or sharing access to goods and services, often facilitated by an online platform. The platform can be commercial, or community based.

All these options have the potential to be sustainable. But this is not a given.

Refitting and maintaining buildings with energy efficient lighting systems by means of a Light as a service (LaaS) provider enables them to be operated more economically using Internet-connected lighting and energy management. Network-as-a-Service (NaaS) is the continuation of the trend towards renting, rather than owning infrastructure and applications.

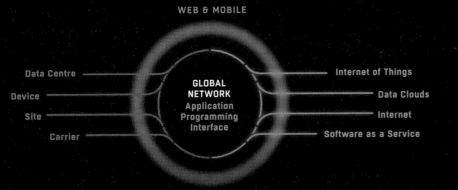

WEB & MOBILE

Data Centre

Device

Site

Carrier

GLOBAL
NETWORK
Application
Programming
Interface

Internet of Things

Data Clouds

Internet

Software as a Service

SOFTWARE

Epsiodes of use

Firstly, and generically, prepare products to be enduring.
Make them resilient and adaptable, no matter what they have
to go through. The point is that affordances remain intact.

Secondly, make them last long, physically, through sufficient
solidity. Provide them with the idea that they're worth feeling
emotionally attached to.

Thirdly think of cats. Cats allegedly have nine lives, depending
on their mythological background.

Products deserve a similar survival capacity. For this we need
a strategic perspective:
• Episode 1: A new product is used for a couple of years.
• Episode 2: There is a new regular owner.
• Episode 3: Another owner. This one takes the object apart for
  refurbishing.
• Episode 4: For you to imagine.

We have to design products for multiple value propositions and
episodes of use in different settings.

Quite adventurous.

A violin can last for more than 200 years, sometimes longer. There's widespread belief among players of stringed musical instruments and experienced listeners that these instruments improve with age and playing. The fame of Stradivarius' instruments is widespread. Yet neither blind experiments nor acoustic analysis have ever found any difference in sound between Stradivarius' violins and comparable high-quality violins from other makers and periods.

Emotional durability

This is the top ambition of many designers: create something with which its owner develops an emotional bond: the evergreen.

Feelings arise, of love, of pride, of responsibility. This is tricky to achieve because it always depends on the owner's personality,
on the owner's previous experience, on the owner's relationships with family and others, and on the owner's wealth.

Yes economics are important: the availability of money reduces the value of possessions. Abundance implies cheapness. Moreover, you can't expect someone to feel attached to every single item in their home. The point is long term use, getting owners to suspend any distrust and to celebrate casual use, with an occasional pinch of satisfaction.

Just being a user and not the owner, as in product-as-a-service models, weakens the bond. It introduces the concept of SEWTCOI: 'Someone Else Will Take Care Of It' and, 'Don't be gentle, it's a rental'.

There is however a phenomenon of a feeling of ownership; it makes you return to 'your own' seat in the theatre, after the break. Bonding happens every day. Use this to fight SEWTCOI.

Moreover, you know about branding. Companies put mountains of effort in brand promotion. Mutual respect between user and the rental brand elongates product lifespan. Products are brand family members.

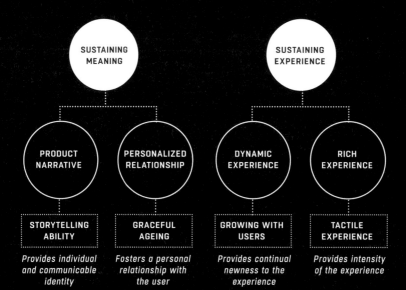

SUSTAINING MEANING		SUSTAINING EXPERIENCE	
PRODUCT NARRATIVE	PERSONALIZED RELATIONSHIP	DYNAMIC EXPERIENCE	RICH EXPERIENCE
STORYTELLING ABILITY	GRACEFUL AGEING	GROWING WITH USERS	TACTILE EXPERIENCE
Provides individual and communicable identity	*Fosters a personal relationship with the user*	*Provides continual newness to the experience*	*Provides intensity of the experience*

Jonathan Chapman wrote a designer's guide to emotionally durable and meaningful products. Below: Hiphop pioneers Run-DMC declared their loyalty to the Adidas Superstars basketball shoes in their 1986 hit 'My Adidas' after which the brand became a hiphop style icon. Keeping trainers in a box and cleaning them with a toothbrush was a thing.

Maintenance and repair

Design for maintenance and repair is picking itself up, dusting itself off, and starting all over again. Maintenance and repair in affluent regions are now uncommon events. Either the work is too time consuming, too expensive, or a replacement is too cheap.

Some future maintenance tasks will happen automatically, like descaling coffeemakers or upgrading software. But, there are grades of difficulty. For some tasks skills are needed, like opening an unruly battery compartment. Endangered chores like polishing shoes depend on knowledge of procedures.

Design for maintenance and repair requires horse sense. You need:

- An understanding of what might be wrong.
- Access.
- Simple disassembly.
- Clear subdivision of parts and modules.
- Safety.
- Coherence (avoid vulnerable spots, such as transitions. between cables and plugs).
- Logic and retraceability.
- Easy reassembly.

You don't want patronizing labels and texts. It's the designer's responsibility that users take good care of their products.

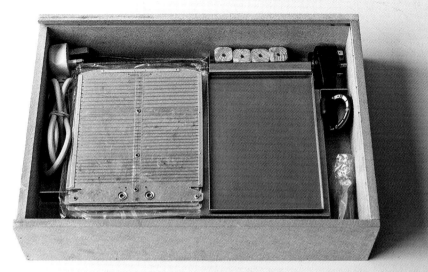

Kasey Hou developed a flat-pack toaster that can be easily repaired. 'If the user can assemble the toaster from scratch, then they feel more comfortable and confident about repairing it because they're familiar with the structure of the toaster and how it works.' Below: Shoes are repairable and can last 20 years. The key is taking care of them.

Refurbishment and remanufacturing

Refurbishment and remanufacturing are happening, but only on a modest scale. They are like repair, but as business-to-business operations, they are more complex.

Refurbishment requires more extended design preparation. Access is required, but in this case, not lay access. Clearly design the borderline between expertise and amateurism.

For professional disassembly you may need uncommon tools. Old components must be replaceable. New components must be compatible. Prepare for future components. They will probably be smaller and more efficient. Energy input may evolve. Monitor changes and failures.

Remanufacturing goes one step deeper. Products are stripped to their core and rebuilt to be as good as new. Consider standardization and compatibility; consider parts harvesting and reuse.

Strategic company commitment is needed to make remanufacturing a success; it's a long-haul process. The old and wise must compete with the new. Time and again, remanufacturing and refurbishment have become a sustainable and a commercial success.

This is how you arrive at products that last.

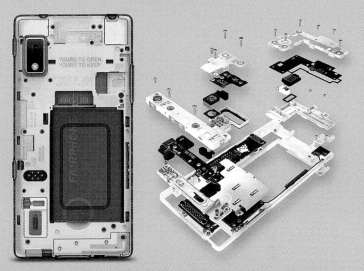

Hundreds of thousands of outdated phones are discarded each day. The Fairphone was designed so that the primary expensive electronics, which don't evolve as rapidly as the phone's other components, are grouped together in a single module. Other modules can be replaced or upgraded. Below: Outdated real estate isn't demolished, but is stripped down and refurbished to avoid the destruction of capital and construction materials.

Disposables

It's hot – buy an ice lolly. Hmm! That's good! Before you know it, you'll just be standing there, eyes looking all over for a bin. Not one within 50 meters. Now what? Drop it and forget. Some products simply are not supposed to last.

• Packaging
• Disposables
• Food

After use, or consumption, they're supposed to disappear, into a basket, or a bag, or a stomach. Often, they don't – even a third of food is wasted.

Some products are supposed to last, but are not very good at that. Things like knickknacks, and clothing items. They are bought without thinking.

They must wait in purgatory – attics, cellars, and wardrobes – to end up in landfill, sometimes even without being unpacked. Oceans are turning into plastic waste accumulators. Organisms have become waste particle containers. Prevention is the obvious way to go, but people are sloppy – we make no time to care.

Legislation works of course, as do regulation and organization. Habits must change.

2.6%

The percentage of global water used for growing cotton.

17-20 %

The estimated percentage of Industrial water pollution that comes from textile dying and treatment.

60,000,000

The estimated number of people who work in the fashion industry worldwide.

700
GALLONS

The amount of water it takes to produce a single cotton T-shirt.

8,000

The estimated number of synthetic chemicals that are used worldwide to turn raw materials into textiles.

92,000,000
TONNES

The amount of waste the fashion industry produces annualy

Some indications of the use of resources and global environmental impact of the fashion industry. Below: Natural branding uses laser-labelling on fruits and vegetables, eliminating paper, glue, and ink on organic produce.

TIPS FOR FURTHER READING (in chronological order)

- **Ellen MacArthur Foundation (2013) TOWARDS THE CIRCULAR ECONOMY VOL. 1; an Economic and Business Rationale for an accelerated Transition.** *Ellen MacArthur Foundation.* Building on Cradle to Cradle but with a stronger business focus, the Ellen MacArthur Foundation popularized the Circular Economy concept with industry leaders and policy makers.

- **Jonathan Chapman (2015) EMOTIONALLY DURABLE DESIGN; Objects, Experiences & Empathy.** *Taylor & Francis.* The book engages with the underlying psychological phenomena that shape patterns of consumption and waste, and defines strategies for the design of products that people want to keep for longer.

- **Conny Bakker, Marcel den Hollander, Ed van Hinte and Yvo Zijlstra (2016) PRODUCTS THAT LAST; Product Design for Circular Business Models.** *BIS Publishers.* Designers and entrepreneurs are little aware of the opportunities that exist in the next product universe, where money is made from products in use, as well as from a product's afterlife.

- **Siem Haffmans, Marjolein van Gelder, Ed van Hinte and Yvo Zijlstra (2018) PRODUCTS THAT FLOW; Circular Business Models and Design Strategies for Fast-Moving Consumer Goods.** *BIS Publishers.* How to deal with fast-moving consumer goods in a more sustainable way?

- **Joe Macleod (2021) ENDINEERING; Designing consumption lifecycles that end as well as they begin.** There is a gap in the consumer lifecycle that needs attention – the end. The book reveals new opportunities and design for better consumer endings.

- **Francesco de Fazio, C. Bakker, B. Flipsen and R. Balkenende (2021) THE DISASSEMBLY MAP: A new method to enhance design for product repairability.** *Journal of Cleaner Production 2021 Vol. 320.* The paper describes the development of a method to visually map the disassembly of a product.

- **Markus Berger, Kate Irvin (eds) (2022) REPAIR: Sustainable Design Futures.** *Routledge.* Repair is an act, metaphor, and foundation for opening up a dialogue about design's role in proposing radically different social, environmental, and economic futures.

- **THE LONG NOW** is a nonprofit established in 01996 to foster long-term thinking. *https://longnow.org.* Famous for The Clock of the Long Now: an immense mechanical instrument, installed in a mountain, designed to keep accurate time for the next 10,000 years.

Salvador Dalí, THE EYE OF SURREALIST TIME (1971). *Dalí had a lifelong obsession with eyes and clocks. We observe reality in perfect time with a resolute 'tick, tick, tick' of the second hand marching inexorably onward. His famous soft watches suggest the collapse of our notions of a fixed cosmic order. Once asked if the soft watches are an unconscious symbol of Albert Einstein's theory of special relativity Dalí denied this stating they were the surrealist perception of a Camembert melting in the sun.*

6. RECYCLING

Recycling is not the panacea to
get us from here to circularity.
It is, however, the final level of the
way back to continuation of use.

The most important design quality
is the potential to salvage used
materials. Track 'm down and
catch 'm, or we will be left with
good for nothing, dirty soup.

Obligatory reprocessing

If we can't avoid making products, they'd better be recyclable. They won't disappear so they must be prepared for continued use, even if it involves breaking them down and recycling the materials.

Recycling boils down to returning materials to as good a condition as possible, ready for reuse. Usually this involves shredding and grinding and a series of complicated reprocessing steps. Things change. The strength, toughness, odor, and color of recycled materials tend to drift away from the original, particularly in plastics. Recycled plastics from household waste are often too tainted for high-end applications.

The good news is, by practicing precautionary product design, we can address this problem. Designers can ensure that materials continue to function in the same or in different products. Well prepared recycling can ensure materials that last.

Success depends on what is achieved in each of three steps:

- Collection
- Sorting
- Reprocessing

Another thought: recycling depends at least as much on return logistics as it does on material composition.

A major challenge in the plastic recycling industry is the efficient separation of plastic waste by type and colour.

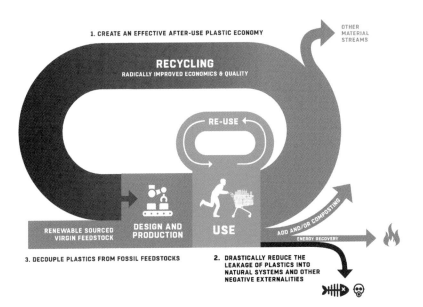

1. CREATE AN EFFECTIVE AFTER-USE PLASTIC ECONOMY

OTHER MATERIAL STREAMS

RECYCLING
RADICALLY IMPROVED ECONOMICS & QUALITY

RE-USE

RENEWABLE SOURCED VIRGIN FEEDSTOCK

DESIGN AND PRODUCTION

USE

AOD AND/OR COMPOSTING

ENERGY RECOVERY

3. DECOUPLE PLASTICS FROM FOSSIL FEEDSTOCKS

2. DRASTICALLY REDUCE THE LEAKAGE OF PLASTICS INTO NATURAL SYSTEMS AND OTHER NEGATIVE EXTERNALITIES

Waste collection

Over here! This is where it all starts anew. Recycling depends on transportation and control of material flows. It's about bringing waste together before getting the most out of it.

Manufacturers collect their process waste to have it recycled; this post-industrial recycling is relatively easy.

In contrast, collecting used products and other waste from people is not. To make post-consumer recycling effective, the public needs to make the first move. They must separate their used leftovers into paper, metal, electronics, glass, textiles, organic waste, and other stuff.

Municipalities (or other organizations) then pick up the waste, providing facilities and transportation.

In Europe, legislation is in place that makes manufacturers responsible for their products when these become waste. There is now a very well-organized waste collection infrastructure.

Nevertheless, separating waste is not easy. Help!

• Does a milk carton belong in the plastics bin?
• Where do I put biodegradable stuff?
• Ancient TL Lamps, what are they?

Designers can help by improving waste's recognizability and directing people to the right bins that swallow it.

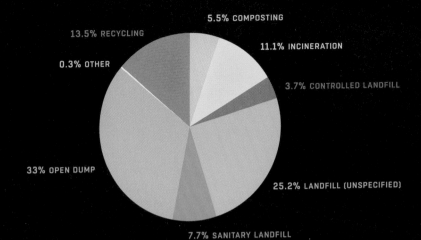

5.5% COMPOSTING

13.5% RECYCLING

11.1% INCINERATION

0.3% OTHER

3.7% CONTROLLED LANDFILL

33% OPEN DUMP

25.2% LANDFILL (UNSPECIFIED)

7.7% SANITARY LANDFILL

The handling of Municipal Solid Waste (MSW) worldwide; only 13.5% gets recycled. Glass is 100% recyclable and can be recycled endlessly without loss of quality or purity. Below: Making glass from cullet needs 30% less energy than using virgin materials. Yet glass from bottles can't be mixed with other types of glass such as windows, crystal, ovenware, Pyrex, and more.

Waste sorting

Once collected, each kind of waste has its own recycling infrastructure.

Glass surrenders to machines. Magnets remove metal caps. Contaminants such as cork, plastic and porcelain are removed by hand or machine. Optical sorting installations separate transparent and colored glass. Let the melting begin!

Mixed plastic household waste like packaging is sorted by hand or machine. The latest innovation is near-infrared spectroscopy (NIR). Each plastic (PET, PP, etc.) has its own fingerprint. NIR spectroscopy machines make it possible to identify and sort different plastics automatically. Compose granules now.

Waste textiles are difficult to sort, as most garments are made of blends of different materials. Manual sorting is often the only reliable way, although NIR spectroscopy is now starting to make its mark. Roughly, the outcome consists of bales of garments of similar materials and colors. Back to future fibers and yarns.

Electric and electronic waste (laptops, phones, TVs, e-vehicles, washing machines, etc.) is a high-value waste stream. Li-ion batteries are hazardous in recycling and need to be processed separately; they are usually removed by hand, together with other valuable components like copper cable.

After cherry picking it's demolition time.

People generate 2.01 billion tons of municipal solid waste annually, with at least 33 percent of that – extremely conservatively – not managed in an environmentally safe manner. Below: The world is on track to generate 2 million-metric-tons of used Li-ion batteries per year that end up as trash. These are valuable and recyclable, yet less than 5% are recycled. (Source: World Bank).

6.4 RECYCLING

Waste decomposition

After painstakingly sorting the different waste streams the next step is remarkably crude.

Most sorted materials are brutally crushed and/or shredded. This is mechanical recycling. Check it out online. A shredding installation is impressive. The procedure is almost painful to watch, considering the sophisticated products that go in there.

What you get is 'fragments' or 'fractions', or 'fibers' (in the case of textiles). For example, let's shred a refrigerator. The fractions consist of a mix of metals, plastics, electronic components, insulation foam, etc. Further sorting is needed-this is called concentration.

A range of machines is available. It's simple physics. Magnets separate iron and steel from the rest. Eddy-current separation uses electromagnetic induction to separate aluminum and copper. Sink-float separation makes higher-density materials sink, and lower-density float, which is handy for separating different plastic fractions.

These are then sorted into the different materials that once constituted a fridge. They will not be 100% pure. A little bit of copper may still be stuck to an aluminum fraction. This copper will be lost when the aluminum is melted into aluminum again. It is what it is.

It will take ages before sorting and reprocessing become as precise as production. That would be a new industrial revolution.

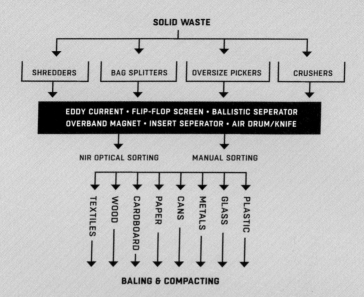

SOLID WASTE

- SHREDDERS
- BAG SPLITTERS
- OVERSIZE PICKERS
- CRUSHERS

EDDY CURRENT • FLIP-FLOP SCREEN • BALLISTIC SEPERATOR
OVERBAND MAGNET • INSERT SEPERATOR • AIR DRUM/KNIFE

NIR OPTICAL SORTING   MANUAL SORTING

- TEXTILES
- WOOD
- CARDBOARD
- PAPER
- CANS
- METALS
- GLASS
- PLASTIC

BALING & COMPACTING

About 450-500 million tonnes of construction and demolition waste is generated every year in Europe, at least a third of which is concrete. Only around a third to two thirds of the waste is recycled. (Source: European Commission).

Chemical recycling

Shredding and reprocessing plastics is detrimental to their molecular health. Recycled plastics often have poorer mechanical properties than new plastics.

Chemical recycling could outperform mechanical processing, which is interesting for a circular economy. The concept is simple. Most plastics are made from raw materials like natural gas and oil, also referred to as 'feedstock'. The oil is refined into ethane and propane, and then treated in a process called 'cracking' to produce ethylene and propylene (monomers). These are then combined to create different polymers, with additives used to create plastics with different properties.

Returning plastics to polymers, monomers, or feedstock, is called chemical recycling. Three routes are being explored:

Dissolution uses heat and solvents to dissolve plastic into a solution of polymers and additives. The additives are separated and the polymer is recovered from the solution. During dissolution the structure of the polymer remains the same.

Depolymerisation (or solvolysis) uses different combinations of chemistry, solvents, and heat to break down polymers into monomers, their building blocks. These are fed back into the normal plastic production process.

Conversion (also pyrolysis or gasification) uses heat and chemistry in a reactor to break down the plastic to oil- or gas-like feedstock (raw material). A refinery or cracker turns the resulting oil or gas into chemicals or plastics.

Dissolution and depolymerisation are in an early stage of development and only happen on a small scale, for instance with polyester. Each polymer needs its own specific treatment. Energy efficiency and toxicity have hardly been considered – there's a long way to go.

Polymer chemists improved an existing polymer by removing a ring at a particular location along the molecule. They then identified two different catalysts that can chemically break down this polymer into constituent monomers with great efficiency (about 85%), at which point the monomers can be reused. (Source: Science, vol. 360, nr. 6387, 2018).

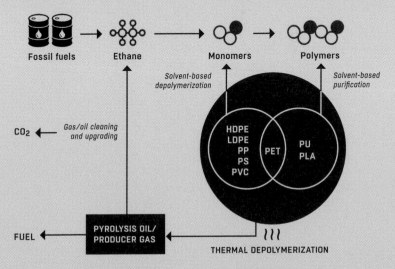

Fossil fuels → Ethane → Monomers → Polymers

CO₂ ← *Gas/oil cleaning and upgrading*

Solvent-based depolymerization

Solvent-based purification

HDPE
LDPE
PP
PS
PVC

PET

PU
PLA

FUEL ← PYROLYSIS OIL/ PRODUCER GAS

THERMAL DEPOLYMERIZATION

Remove poison

Plastics can be improved to provide extra functionality through additives.

There are additives to keep out UV light, keep in moisture, stop micro-organisms, provide a rubbery feeling, contain energy, produce foam, enhance smoothness, insulate, enhance stiffness, improve plasticity in the mold, provide better wear resistance, improve electrical or heat conduction, and even, believe it or not, change color. Over 10,000 different additives have been identified.

Some of these substances have been in use for a long time but have proven to be toxic: substances of concern (SOC) or persistent organic pollutants (POP). Manufacturers have stopped using many SOCs and POPs, but they are still around: legacy additives. They can be found in recycled plastics. Recycling spreads the danger, which is not what we want. Remove the 'poison' before recycling is the message.

Substituting an additive for a less toxic one can have interesting side effects. The old (toxic) bromide flame retardant additives were replaced by phosphate flame retardants. Suddenly the sink-float separation no longer worked: bromide flame retardants increase plastic density, phosphate flame retardants, however, don't. The recycler could no longer distinguish between plastics treated with flame retardants and those that weren't – not good for the recycling business.

We really should ban toxic chemicals and try to find creative design solutions instead. Help is needed to deal with the inevitable trade-offs.

Flame retardant additives add product safety but can make plastics more difficult to recycle.
Below: European production of plastic packaging with additives (source: Frost & Sullivan)

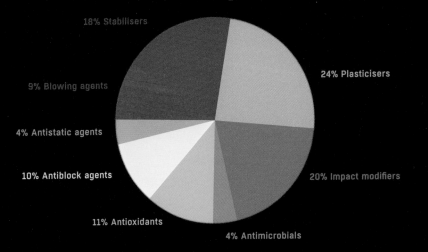

18% Stabilisers

24% Plasticisers

9% Blowing agents

4% Antistatic agents

10% Antiblock agents

20% Impact modifiers

11% Antioxidants

4% Antimicrobials

6.7 RECYCLING
Biobased plastics

In the case of plastics, the word 'biobased' can be ambiguous. Biobased plastics are made from plants and other biomass like algae but this by no means entails that they are biodegradable. Only some are. Here we have a greenwashing selling point.

Drop in please! Most petroleum-based plastics have a biobased chemical equivalent. Same material, different source. They're called drop-in biobased plastics.

As materials, biobased plastics are sustainable, well sort of. When incinerated (or composted, in the case of the biodegradable variants) they are carbon neutral.

Yes - carbon neutral: plants store CO_2 when they grow. Using these plants to produce biobased plastics removes CO_2 from the atmosphere and keeps it stored throughout the entire product life. The amount of CO_2 emitted to the atmosphere by burning bioplastics is equal to the amount stored by the plants.

However, in the broader context there are some issues. Land use might compete with food production; harvesting and processing still use fossil energy; and biodegradables may contaminate recycling flows. But there's rapid development in this field. Some biobased plastics have unique properties and may even outperform the petroleum-based originals.

Choose biobased materials with recovery in mind. Renewable isn't everything - the long term is.

Ecovative developed Mycofoam, made from agricultural waste placed into molds and mixed with live mycelium fungus, which essentially grows the material into a finished shape that can be dried and used as a stable packaging material. German company Qmilch uses milk that would otherwise have been thrown away to create textile fibers.

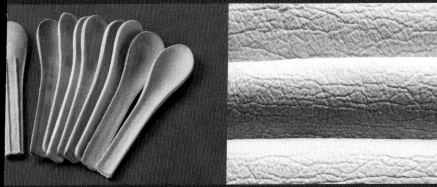

Bakeys is an Indian company that developed edible spoons made from sorghum flour that come in three flavors: plain, sweet and savory. Piñatex, manufactured by Ananas Anam, is a durable alternative to leather, made from pineapple leaves.

Party supplies derived from the leaves of the areca palm, left over during the production of betel nut in India. Biodegradable plastics can be decomposed by the action of living organisms, usually microbes, into water, carbon dioxide, and biomass. Bottle designed by Ari Jónsson.

Biodegradables

Biomaterials show that there is life after death. Wood, bone, skin, wool, cork, cotton, bamboo, and many other fibers have been turned into objects, tools, and garments for ages. They will rot unless a coating prevents that from happening. Rotting is being eaten.

Biodegradation is about being eaten by small organisms. In the process they produce CO_2 or methane (CH_4), depending on whether oxygen is present.

Biodegradation can occur spontaneously, for instance in the compost heap in your garden, if you can afford a garden (and know how to build a compost heap).

Biodegradation can also happen under industrial conditions. Waste is collected in large volumes, mixed with nitrogen-rich materials and carbon-rich leaves, branches, and paper to ensure the right processing balance. The mixture is watered every day. In addition, air can be pumped through the mix.

Some packaging materials are labelled 'biodegradable'. In many cases they are biodegradable, in the industrial sense. But they're usually not the spontaneous micro-organism feeder. Biodegradation in outdoor conditions is often far from complete. Bits of undigested plastics remain.

So, who wouldn't be confused about biodegradability? Consumers throw 'biodegradables' in parks and on the pavement, unwittingly polluting the world with microplastics. Manufacturers also struggle to understand biodegradability. European standards try to help by setting an official time limit for biodegradability. Designers have to clarify breakdown principles, for everyone to understand.

Biodegradable & compostable products

Bioplastics granulates

Bio refinery

ORGANIC RECYCLING

Biowaste bin

Plant fertilizer

Bio-gas

Seperate collection of waste

Biowaste treatment industrial compost plant

Indonesian based start-up Avani has developed a 100% biodegradable replacement for plastic bags that dissolves in water.

6.9 RECYCLING

Avoid incineration

Landfills take space. The potential is limited. The best way to stop waste increase is to stop producing it.

A common way to get rid of waste is to burn it. There is a euphemism for that: thermal recycling. The principle is that the energy recovered from burning waste is used to generate electricity and heat, which can then be used to heat homes. The rationale is that useless waste is used and thus 'contributes to the circular economy'. Nevertheless, materials disappear and carbon dioxide escapes. We have a leak.

In some instances, burning waste is necessary:

- Biohazardous waste (for instance from hospitals) must be destroyed.
- Composite materials can become a nuisance.

In any case it's worth considering the pros and cons of incineration. Burning bio-based materials releases the previously absorbed CO_2, for new plants, trees, and algae to absorb it once more, etc. In Europe this process is considered carbon neutral.

But perhaps any non-metabolic process that emits CO_2 must be avoided.

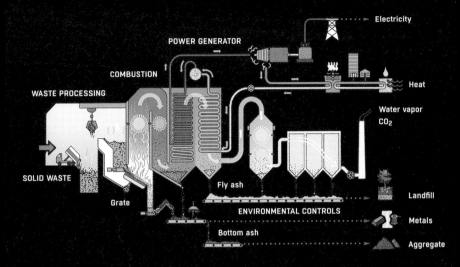

POWER GENERATOR

COMBUSTION

WASTE PROCESSING

Electricity

Heat

Water vapor
CO_2

SOLID WASTE

Fly ash

Grate

Landfill

ENVIRONMENTAL CONTROLS

Metals

Bottom ash

Aggregate

Incineration with energy recovery is the combustion of waste under controlled conditions to generate electricity and/or heat. It is an expensive technology and is mostly used in high-income countries. (source: World Bank)

Keep it separable and traceable

The main rule, in the widest sense is: Don't mess things up, literally. This implies an obvious but not yet conventional principle: Keep materials separable and traceable for years on end.

Thus, a new angle for functional integration is: it's not necessarily smart to try and put all you need into one super material that you'd then have to incinerate after use. Always consider what happens in the long run.

Design for recycling boils down to:

- Make high-value or hazardous components easy to access and remove.
- Use recycled materials that can be recycled.
- Use material combinations and connections that will separate during recycling (no glue).
- Don't use hazardous substances.

Sustainability will keep you off the streets for a lifetime.

Swiss comedian Ursus Wehrli loves organisation in the extreme. In his book 'The Art of Clean Up', Wehrli arranges our chaotic world into neat rows sorted by colour, size, shape or type.

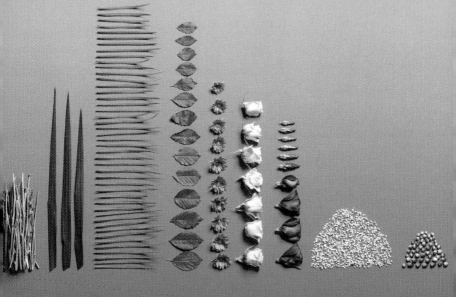

TIPS FOR FURTHER READING (in chronological order)

- **Rachel Carson (1962) SILENT SPRING** *Houghton Mifflin Publishers.* The book documents the adverse environmental effects caused by pesticides. Carson accuses the chemical industry of intentionally spreading disinformation and public officials of accepting industry claims uncritically. Predictably, the chemical industry fiercely criticized the book.

- **Michael F. Ashby (2016) MATERIALS AND SUSTAINABLE DEVELOPMENT** *Elsevier.* The book provides a structure and framework for analyzing sustainable development and the role of materials in it. It recognizes the complexity inherent in discussions on sustainability and shows how to deal with it in a systematic way.

- **Helene Wiesinger, Zhanyun Wang, and Stefanie Hellweg (2021) DEEP DIVE INTO PLASTIC MONOMERS, ADDITIVES, AND PROCESSING AIDS** *Environmental Science & Technology 55 (13), 9339-9351.* Only a limited number of the wide range of chemical substances in plastics have been researched. The study identifies over 2400 substances of potential concern: there are worries about their persistence, bioaccumulation, and toxicity.

- **Jelle Joustra and Riel Bessai (2021) CIRCULAR COMPOSITES: a design guide for products containing composite materials in a circular economy** *Free download through https://books.open.tudelft.nl/home/ catalog/book/23.* Composites are increasingly used to optimize the performance of products. This is great, but the end-of-life of composites is often problematic. The book provides design guidelines for circular strategies, ranging from reuse to restructuring and recycling.

- **DESIGN FOR RECYCLING, Design from Recycling; Practical Guidelines for Designers (2021) PolyCE.** *Free download from polyce-project.eu.* With a focus on electrical and electronic equipment, this guide provides helpful checklists and case studies of designing with recycled materials and designing products to be better recyclable.

- **EUROPEAN NORMS FOR BIODEGRADABLE PLASTICS: CEN/TR 159325 and ISO 18606.** There are more norms and standards underway, dealing with all manners of composting and recycling of biobased and biodegradable plastics.

Cornelia Parker COLD DARK MATTER: AN EXPLODED VIEW (1991) *Parker's art is about destruction, resurrection, and reconfiguration. Just as the Big Bang was a creative event, Parker's 'exploded' works provide the viewer with a new way to experience an object through destruction. The real test of life is breath – the perfect cycle of inhale and exhale, with tiny little deaths on either end. Parker finds the breath of things and removes whatever obstructs it.*

7. BETTER BUSINESS

Watch our supply chains continuously extending over continents and oceans. They're getting ever more entangled.

They have also become increasingly vulnerable to disasters: climate changes, water disappears, toxin levels rise, life becomes extinct.

People take wrong turns, and serious accidents happen. We engage in conflicts and mis-underestimate the side-effects of our actions. We know all this. Risks increase. Unveiling itself is the riskiness of scale. Risk is probability x impact. Both are on the increase.

Companies need to prepare for this. Increasingly they do so by embracing principles of sustainability.

Stay alert

Business risk is traditionally financial. It concerns return on investment. An initiative is set in motion and usually, in a couple of years, its success is known: it is either profitable or not. After that there's a scenario of optimization, until the market is satisfied.

A new initiative is called for. The drill is familiar.

Sustainable business risks are different. They manifest themselves over a longer period. Energy availability, legislation, material flows, new responsibilities: these risks affect businesses on many dimensions. Largely they are outside the organization's estimated control.

Some things you can foresee, such as demographics and climate change. Other things you can specifically prepare for: pandemics, floods. But don't neglect the unexpected. Stay alert. By the way, not all change is disastrous.

Managing risk requires early investment decisions, long-term capacity building, and of course being prepared to adapt. Things will never be the same.

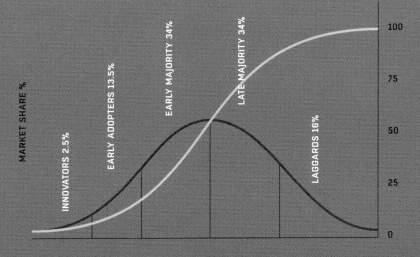

The diffusion of innovations according to Rogers (1962). With successive groups of consumers adopting the new technology (shown in blue), its market share (yellow) will eventually reach the saturation level. Rogers proposes that five main elements influence the spread of a new idea: the innovation itself, adopters, communication channels, time, and a social system. This process relies heavily on social capital. The innovation must be widely adopted in order to self-sustain.

Sense the potential

This is the current idea: Human effort adds value to what is readily and freely available, like water. This's not fair – adding value always comes at the expense of other value. We exhaust and pollute resources.

For instance: conversion of solar energy requires mining to produce equipment and infrastructure, which takes space. Nothing is free.

It is, however, wrong to consider adding value and sustainability as opposites. Consider this: producing a sustainable future also adds value.

The deeper cause of this mistake is that in economic thinking, value is often confused with certain amounts of money, even though that is just one expression of it, specifically the kind used in transactions. Consequently, dealings that are strictly financial are believed to add value. Well, they may do the opposite. The simplest example is a company that buys back stock from shareholders. In that way they prevent money from being invested in innovation and production capacity. Value is extracted.

Another form of transaction thinking brings us to developing products that may sell, but that don't add value to life. It's worth considering why you're tempting customers to purchase something if it's detrimental to sustainability.
Value is a sense of potential.

'A cynic is someone who knows the price of everything and the value of nothing.'
OSCAR WILDE, 1854-1900.

Enhance shared value

Shared value creation is the aim of sustainable businesses. We benefit from a shared sense of potential.

The bare minimum is that sustainable trade does not harm people and resources; nobody and nothing shall be worse off within a lifetime. At best businesses create value for all: customers, employees, shareholders, supply chain exploiters, society, and life on the planet.

Sustainability includes investments. Companies have a social and environmental impact because of what they do. They steer processing, transport, trade, and behavior. That's where you can improve environmental, social and governance performance. These are all rapidly becoming design considerations.

The shared value of sustainability emerges from continually working with and learning from all those who have an interest in sustainable development.

Investing in sustainability helps manage risks. The value of sustainability also drives innovation. Designing products and services to meet and exceed environmental standards or social needs is profitable; if not in the short term, then in the long term. Profits allow investments in enhancing shared value.

A symbiotic relationship is two organisms benefitting from each other, like the classic example of the anemone and the clownfish. The anemone provides the clownfish with protection and shelter, while the clownfish provides the anemone with nutrients in the form of waste while also scaring off potential predator fish. Below: Every purchase matters in the lives of others. Oeko-Tex is a label for textiles tested for harmful substances. If a product carries a Standard 100 label, it is harmless for human health.

7.4 BETTER BUSINESS
Set ambitious goals

Here we have the World Business Council for Sustainable Development. This is a community of over 200 leading businesses, led by a CEO. They work as a collective 'to accelerate the system transformations needed for a net zero, nature positive, and more equitable future'.

They ask their members to adhere to 5 criteria:

1. Set an ambition to reach net zero greenhouse gas emissions, no later than 2050 and have a science-informed plan to achieve it.

2. Set ambitious, short and mid-term environmental goals that contribute to nature and biodiversity recovery by 2050.

3. Have a policy in place to respect human rights and declare support for the UN Guiding Principles on Business and Human Rights.

4. Declare support for inclusion, equality, diversity, and the elimination of any form of discrimination.

5. Operate at the highest level of transparency by disclosing material sustainability.

Criteria such as these also challenge designers. They can explore new partnerships, refocus creativity, and search for new areas for development of products, services, materials, and processes. Net-zero greenhouse emissions are the classic goal. Ways to contribute to biodiversity recovery is as yet uncharted territory.

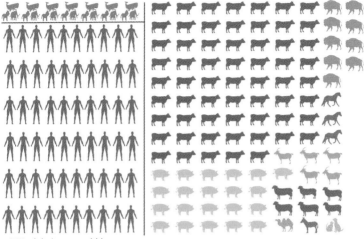

WILD MAMMALS
4% global mammal biomass

LIVESTOCK & PETS
62% global mammal biomass

34% global mammal biomass
HUMANS

In 2019, about 43.1 billion tons of CO_2 from human activities were emitted into the atmosphere. Global livestock contributed 7.1 billion tons. Reductions of 55% before 2030 are needed to limit the rise in global temperature to 1.5 degrees.

Greenwash

There are other companies – many of them. They understand the value of a reputation of engagement with sustainability all too well. In addition, they often recognize public misunderstandings concerning sustainability. They recognize opportunities to present themselves as 'green'. We call this 'greenwashing'.

It leads to many superficial, unsubstantiated, or misleading claims:

Recycling is good
Our material can be recycled > *yes, but does it happen?*
Our material has been recycled > *yes, but what comes next?*

Vegetables are healthy
Our snacks contain vegetables.
> *the point is reduction of calories.*
Our product contains no E-numbers.
> *the E-number of oxygen is E 948.*

Electricity is clean
An electric cooker is clean.
> *that heavily depends on production and efficiency.*
This SUV is green .
> *is that so? Why does it weigh 20 times your body?*

Our textiles are green
Our materials are sustainable.
> *production and labor conditions are part of it.*
We take back used clothes > *how often does this happen?*

We are so green
We are climate neutral > *is that even possible?*
Our logo is green > *congratulations!*

You could say everything is natural and biodegradable, as long as you don't mention how many centuries it takes to decompose. Below: Colored nylon nets make fruit look more natural and fresher.

TIPS FOR FURTHER READING (in chronological order)

- **Paul Hawken, Amory B. Lovins, L. Hunter Lovins (2000) NATURAL CAPITALISM: Creating the next Industrial Revolution.** *Back Bay Books.* The book makes an argument for 'a new type of industrialism' that is both more efficient and profitable, while simultaneously protecting the planet and creating jobs.

- **Thomas Princen (2005) THE LOGIC OF SUFFICIENCY.** *MIT Press.* What if modern society took ecological constraint as a given, not a hindrance but a source of long-term economic security? How would it organize itself, structure its industry, shape its consumption?

- **Mariana Mazzucato (2019) THE VALUE OF EVERYTHING; Making and Taking in the Global Economy.** *Penguin Books Ltd.* In modern capitalism, value-extraction is rewarded more highly than value-creation. We misidentify taking with making and have lost sight of what value really means.

- **Nada R. Sanders and John D. Wood (2019) FOUNDATIONS OF SUSTAINABLE BUSINESS: Theory, Function, and Strategy.** *2ⁿᵈ Edition. Wiley.* Helps students understand how leadership, finance, accounting, risk management, supply chain management and operations can be adapted to meet the sustainability goals of the 21ˢᵗ century.

- **Anna Lowenhaupt Tsing (2021) THE MUSHROOM AT THE END OF THE WORLD; On the Possibility of Life in Capitalist Ruins.** *Princeton University Press.* The Mushroom at the End of the World delves into the relationship between capitalist destruction and collaborative survival within multispecies landscapes, the prerequisite for continuing life on earth.

- **WORLD BUSINESS COUNCIL FOR SUSTAINABLE DEVELOPMENT.** *wbcsd.org.* A global, CEO-led community of over 200 of the world's leading sustainable businesses. With strategic information and tools for companies starting the transition to a sustainable business.

- **HOW TO BUILD A SUSTAINABILITY FOCUSED VALUE PROPOSITION STATEMENT?** *explorerlabs.co.* Sustainability focused value proposition statements are important for sustainable innovation concepts because they are complex and involve many ecosystem stakeholders. The site provides a helpful step-by-step tool.

Jenny Holzer, TRUISMS (from 1977). *Jenny Holzer could be described as an artist for whom words are images. She became known in New York City in 1977 for inexpensively printed T-shirts, postcards and anonymously posted sheets of text known as Truisms; more than 250 cryptic maxims, terse commands, and shrewd observations. In 1982 she projected her Truisms on the enormous Spectacolor LED board in Times Square, with smaller scrolling signs to evoke the digital clocks and screens through which we are continuously fed information (and told what to think) in urban environments. All the texts are phrased in ways that make them seem private and public, solitary and shared. There may be so many voices in a work that the point of view is impossible to determine.*

ABUSE OF POWER SHOULD COME AS NO SURPRISE
ALIENATION CAN PRODUCE ECCENTRICS OR REVOLUTIONARIES
AN ELITE IS INEVITABLE
ANGER OR HATE CAN BE A USEFUL MOTIVATING FORCE
ANY SURPLUS IS IMMORAL
DISGUST IS THE APPROPRIATE RESPONSE TO MOST SITUATIONS
EVERYONE'S WORK IS EQUALLY IMPORTANT
EXCEPTIONAL PEOPLE DESERVE SPECIAL CONCESSIONS
FAITHFULNESS IS A SOCIAL NOT A BIOLOGICAL LAW
FREEDOM IS A LUXURY NOT A NECESSITY
GOVERNMENT IS A BURDEN ON THE PEOPLE
HUMANISM IS OBSOLETE
IDEALS ARE EVENTUALLY REPLACED BY CONVENTIONAL GOALS
INHERITANCE MUST BE ABOLISHED
KILLING IS UNAVOIDABLE BUT IS NOTHING TO BE PROUD OF
LABOR IS A LIFE-DESTROYING ACTIVITY
MONEY CREATES TASTE
MORALS ARE FOR LITTLE PEOPLE
MOST PEOPLE ARE NOT FIT TO RULE THEMSELVES
MOSTLY YOU SHOULD MIND YOUR OWN BUSINESS
MUCH WAS DECIDED BEFORE YOU WERE BORN
MURDER HAS ITS SEXUAL SIDE
PAIN CAN BE A VERY POSITIVE THING
PEOPLE ARE NUTS IF THEY THINK THEY CONTROL THEIR LIVES
PEOPLE WHO DON'T WORK WITH THEIR HANDS ARE PARASITES
PEOPLE WHO GO CRAZY ARE TOO SENSITIVE
PEOPLE WON'T BEHAVE IF THEY HAVE NOTHING TO LOSE
PLAYING IT SAFE CAN CAUSE A LOT OF DAMAGE
PRIVATE OWNERSHIP IS AN INVITATION TO DISASTER
ROMANTIC LOVE WAS INVENTED TO MANIPULATE WOM
SELFISHNESS IS THE MOST BASIC MOTIVATION
SEPARATISM IS THE WAY TO A NEW BEGINNING
SEX DIFFERENCES ARE HERE TO STAY

8. SUSTAINING SOFTWARE

The sheer amount of data that our systems process is far larger than humanity can ever come to terms with. Energy consumption is soaring, and this is only gradually getting noticed. Data centers are a silent bunch.

Interrelationship between hardware and software power is driving an upward running spiral of increasing deceptive perfection. It's not that complicated to dampen these effects, all it needs is care.

Red hot data

Take a selfie and put it online. There's a selfie index, based on careful assumptions. One selfie contains 2 MB. The index is the amount of CO_2 emissions per MB. The emissions from 10 selfies on the internet equal driving 1 kilometer with a normal car. Consider this: in 2020 we humans shot 93 million selfies a day worldwide. That's just selfies – a fragment of all software.

Life without software just isn't life. Software is in an intimate embrace with hardware. Gee up! The hardware gains speed and capacity. Eat! Software employs it all and wants more.

Growing data swarms need a soaring amount of energy. Software has a huge impact on energy consumption; it determines what servers and storage drivers do. The more they do, the more cooling they need.

Cooling is undercover inefficiency.

The University of Cambridge estimates that the Bitcoin network swallows 126 Terawatt-hours (TWh). Switzerland swallows half of that; soon it will be entire Brazil.

Artificial Intelligence is just as hot. The wasteful approach of throwing more computing power at a problem to refine results has been dubbed 'red AI'.

Waste heat recovery from data centers is bound to play an important role for the energy transition, as almost 100% of the electricity supply to a data center is transformed into heat. The old server population is estimated to consume 96% of server energy but to deliver only 4% of performance capacity. Below: Since 2010, the number of internet users worldwide has doubled, while global internet traffic has expanded 15-fold (source: IEA).

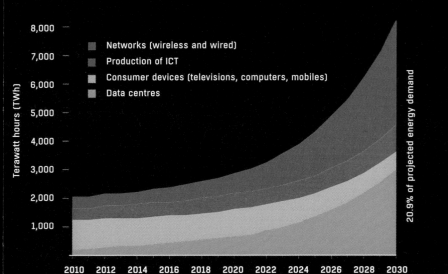

Orders of effects

Faster, smaller, cheaper are the driving forces of technological development. Technology's wish is to disappear. Software is invisible anyway, but it has three orders of effects on sustainability:

Immediate effects: are caused by production, use, and disposal of software products and services. Software and product lifespan have a mutual influence. The elderly program glides into slowness. It takes costly effort to update it and add features. Before you know it, hardware is no longer capable of handling enhancements. But hey! Here's some fresh hardware, new and improved. New features are not necessarily convenient – they may only be different.

Enabling effects: concern what an application is meant for over time. This includes opportunities to consume less or more, speed, lighting, HD streaming, you name it. Consider 'intuitive' versus frustration and system condescendence. The latter lead to more energy consumption. Changes induced by system use, such as sharing, or performance deals are part of it. Here software helps to create a sustainable environment. Software can help run sustainable businesses, organizations, education, and healthcare. Software for sustainability!

Structural effects: these influence culture over a longer period. They emerge from ongoing use of software systems. Look at computerized bureaucracy and social networking and what they entail for energy consumption. Software changes the world forever.

Mycelium threads branch out under the forest floor, connecting the roots of distant trees in what scientists have dubbed the 'wood-wide-web', distributing both nutrients like carbon and signals. Below: Part of the New York City Police Department's surveillance machinery. The higher the proportion of non-white residents, the higher the concentration of facial recognition compatible CCTV cameras. (Amnesty International)

Main principles

Try to:

- Estimate the long-term effects of design decisions.

- Trust the human scale and build from there. Stay small unless you need to grow big.

- Encourage trustful systems. Or dissuade paranoia.

- Always have skin in the game and ask the same from partners and customers.

- Codify positive human values in lowest-level services.

- Pursue algorithmic transparency.

- Use smart tech and AI platforms to elevate and augment, not replace us.

- Understand the impact of new affordances on our minds and mental health.

- Avoid manipulative tricks that exploit our lower-level brain functions.

- Not check these principles on Google or TikTok.

- Not order a pizza.

The number of smartphone subscriptions worldwide today surpasses six billion. 70% of web traffic happens on a mobile device. The average time spent on smartphones is 171 mins per day.

MOBLIE DEVICES, LAPTOPS, TABLETS

AUTOMOBILES

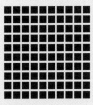

Annual production weight in metric tons

1 black block = 1 million

Exajoules of primary energy required for manufactoring (1 black block = 1 exajoule)

Average product life expectancy in years (1 black block = 1 year)

Amount of energy used per year (1 black block = 0.1 exajoule)

8.4 SUSTAINING SOFTWARE
All's well that ends well

In September 2018, thinkers and doers convened from
all around the world to define instructions, good advice,
provocations, and rules, to build tech products, start-ups, and
communities. They sent a clear signal of actively to breaking
with the Silicon Valley-monoculture. The creators describe
tech products as:

• Tools.
• Made by humans.
• For makers, not for what's made.
• Meant to be owned.
• Built for engagement, empowerment, and regular exercise
  (Take them out for a RUN every now and then!)
• Needing fresh air and light.

Software is written as an entry to eternity. Putting an end to
drifting code is very hard. How easy it is to get a subscription
online, and how hard to end it. (Try leaving Facebook!).

The right to be forgotten (RTBF) is often overlooked.
Offboarding, both digitally and physically, should be given
more attention in design. Quitting is an essential part of any
economy that strives to be more circular and sustainable.

René Magritte: 'If the dream is a translation of waking life – waking life is also a translation of the dream.' (Décalcomanie, 1966). Below: 150 guiding principles for everyone who shapes technology today and a new direction for a tech industry that is slowly waking up to its societal challenges. ('The Copenhagen Catalog', 2018)

TIPS FOR FURTHER READING (in chronological order)

- **Lorenz M. Hilty and Bernard Aebischer (2015) ICT FOR SUSTAINABILITY: An Emerging Research Field.** *In: Hilty, L., Aebischer, B. (eds) ICT Innovations for Sustainability. Advances in Intelligent Systems and Computing, vol 310. Springer, Cham.* The introduction chapter to this book describes a three-levels model with first-, second- and third-order effects of ICT on the environment, which allows us to view ICT as both part of the problem and part of the solution.

- **Joe Macleod (2017) ENDS: Why we overlook endings for humans, products, services and digital. And why we shouldn't.** *Closureexperiences. com.* Nearly 30 years of Climate Change discussion and we still fail to accept the implications of ending our carbon consumption. In a world awash with start-ups and new tech, this book tells you why it's critical we start considering endings.

- **Aimee van Wynsberghe (2021) SUSTAINABLE AI: AI for sustainability and the sustainability of AI.** *AI and Ethics 1, 213-218.* The author defines sustainable AI as a movement to foster change in the entire lifecycle of AI products (i.e., idea generation, training, re-tuning, implementation, governance) towards greater ecological integrity and social justice.

- **International Energy Agency IEA (2021) DATA CENTRES AND DATA TRANSMISSION NETWORKS.** *Tracking report, available through iea.org.* Data centers account for around 1% of global electricity demand, with demand for data services rising exponentially. The good news is that ICT companies are also major purchasers of renewable energy.

- **GREEN SOFTWARE FOUNDATION** *https://greensoftware.foundation/* The Green Software Foundation's mission is to minimize carbon and maximize trust. Go there for Principles of Green Software Engineering.

- **BITCOIN ENERGY CONSUMPTION INDEX** *https://digiconomist.net/ bitcoin-energy-consumption/* The Index provides the latest estimate of the total energy consumption of the Bitcoin network.

Nam June Paik, TV BUDDHA (1974 /2002). *A Buddha from the 18th century posed with a symbolic hand gesture called 'mudra' – for tranquil meditation – is placed in front of a video camera, recording the statue while playing this projected image on a tv screen. This work induces the feeling that the Buddha is doomed to be forever caught in the closed-circuit loop that is the infinite play of his reflection on the TV screen. This encompasses themes such as the hold of screens on society. It also juxtaposes modernization and emerging technologies with religious and historical themes and conveys the vanity of modern times, with the Buddha contemplating and absorbed in his own image like society's self-absorption, which is driven by the media and technology. Another message is that of surveillance – with the Buddha watching himself and an audience viewing.*

9. MEASURING EFFECTS

When you've made the proverbial difference, you need proof. The main method for providing proof is Life Cycle Assessment (LCA). This is easier for technology than for social circumstances.

LCA works best when comparisons with predecessors are available.

Results heavily depend on assumptions. That's OK; design always does. The point is to be aware of this and to be transparent.

Be cautious of assumptions

You'd love to know the difference you made for sustainability, wouldn't you? Just to be sure. There are measuring methods. Life Cycle Assessment (LCA) is the most influential. Always remember that LCA's based on built-in assumptions and:

Garbage in = garbage out. The quality of the outcome depends on data quality.

There is no certainty. There is only probability. Data can never capture all the specifics and idiosyncrasies of your project. Conclusions feed on bits of speculation.

Mind sensitivity. Analyze different scenarios and look at change in the outcomes. It may help prioritize ideas in your design efforts.

Understand your method. There's always a manual – this time read it. Terrible errors in judgement have been made by those mindlessly applying LCAs.

Be critical of your results. A bias may sneak in. You secretly want that cardboard packaging to be 'better' than the plastic alternative and voila, it is. Have someone look at your data and assumptions. Or question yourself.

And question LCAs by others. Who paid for a study? Could the client have influenced the outcome? Is it robust enough to support a redesign case?

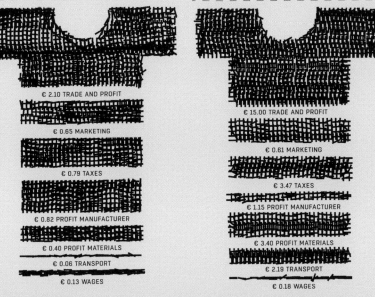

€ 4.99
FAST FASHION T-SHIRT

€ 2.10 TRADE AND PROFIT

€ 0.65 MARKETING

€ 0.79 TAXES

€ 0.82 PROFIT MANUFACTURER

€ 0.40 PROFIT MATERIALS

€ 0.06 TRANSPORT

€ 0.13 WAGES

€ 29.00
MID PRICE T-SHIRT

€ 15.00 TRADE AND PROFIT

€ 0.61 MARKETING

€ 3.47 TAXES

€ 1.15 PROFIT MANUFACTURER

€ 3.40 PROFIT MATERIALS

€ 2.19 TRANSPORT

€ 0.18 WAGES

The production costs of a T-shirt have plummeted to fifty cents. Under which conditions these products are assembled and where the cotton comes from remains unclear. Below: Millions of items of brand-new unsold or returned stock is destroyed every year.

Life Cycle Assessment

Life Cycle Assessment concerns the environmental impact of a product or service over all stages of its life cycle. LCA procedures are documented in an official standard (ISO 14040). They take four steps:

Goal and Scope: define the product and/or service you want to measure, and which part of the life cycle you want to focus on. Also, decide which processes to include in your analysis.

Life Cycle Inventory: collect and structure the necessary data, for instance the bill of materials, energy use, or the input and output of the system you want to investigate.

Impact Assessment: translate your data to impacts, using a suitable database, for instance through www.openlca.org. You can for instance measure the impact of your product or system in terms of global warming potential (CO_2).

Interpretation: search for meaning; try to translate results into action.

For designers, a fast-track LCA sometimes is enough. Using existing LCA software, designers can make quick estimates of environmental impacts and drive their design process forward. When doing a fast-track LCA, keep the five rules (9.1) in mind.

LCAs tend to look at the past. They start with what we already have and aim at optimization. Designers prefer to ask questions about the future. Use LCA to establish a benchmark and a point of departure, and don't get stuck in optimization mode.

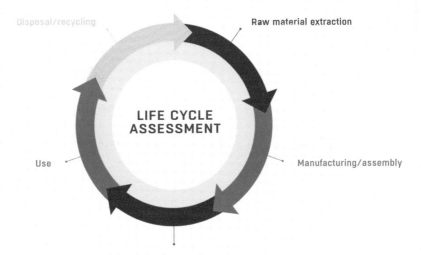

Disposal/recycling

Raw material extraction

LIFE CYCLE ASSESSMENT

Use

Manufacturing/assembly

Transportation & distribution

Hyperloop technology has the potential to transport goods and people at rapid speeds between cities. The transport system involves building a complex infrastructure. At present we're still struggling with comfort and safety issues for people transport. It's not yet certain that Hyperloop will be more energy efficient than high-speed rail.

Social Life Cycle Assessment

If you create a carbon neutral, fully biodegradable product produced under horrible, inhumane conditions, is that a sustainable design?

No.

There is much more to sustainability than environmental impact.
The Sustainable Development Goals stress the importance of social and societal issues, such as zero hunger and reduced inequalities. But measuring social and societal impact is not simple.

Social LCAs look at workers, consumers, local community, society, and assess topics such as child labor, health & safety, local employment, cultural heritage, corruption, fair competition, and much more.

There currently are no reliable databases for a Social LCA, and the methodology is still under development. Nevertheless, even simply listing possible effects, attention points and risks can be a big step forward when planning implementation of a sustainable product or service. You have to wonder: whose lifecycle needs to be assessed?

Burning cables to recover copper at the Agbogbloshie e-waste landfill, Accra, Ghana.

2003

2013

Chilean architect Alejandro Aravena created affordable, fully functional 'half houses' for residents to expand using their own labor and skill. Below: Fashion Revolution strives towards changing the way clothing is sourced, produced and consumed.

I made this for
$0,60

I bought this for
$50

Rebound and spill-over

Life cycle assessments measure first-order effects. These are the direct environmental and social impacts of a product or service on the environment, and on people.

Second-order effects (rebound and spill-over effects) take more time to come to light and occur on a larger scale. 'Rebound effects' are the bad guys.

Reducing car travel may save money. Spending this on other goods and services may require more energy than the car did at first. When people feel they have 'done their bit' for the environment in energy and time, they often reward themselves with more consumption.

As a result, improvements in material or energy efficiency result in smaller than expected reductions in the consumption of energy and material resources – or even in an overall net increase.

Fortunately, there are also 'spill-over effects': an environmental behavior triggers positive changes in other behaviors. You buy an energy efficient fridge. You start wondering about the energy consumption of other appliances. Consequentially in the future you only buy the most efficient ones. You may get serious about solar panels and get rid of the car.

Both 'rebound' and 'spill over' account for prior behavior influencing what happens next. Designers should be aware of these evident cliff-hangers and try to incorporate them.

Our desire to see the world causes nearly 10% of all greenhouse-gas emissions. People who see themselves as leading sustainable lifestyles are often the most carbon-intensive. Below: Rebound effects illustrated: appliances get more energy efficient while homes get more gadgets, more screens and new TVs get bigger, causing overall energy consumption to rise.

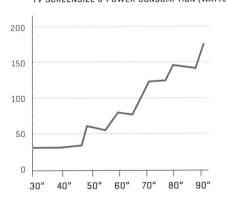

ENERGY CONSUMPTION OF APPLIANCES (%)

Airconditioners

Refrigerators

Clothes washers

TV SCREENSIZE & POWER CONSUMPTION (WATTS)

Indicators, targets, goals

How can we aim for a more sustainable future, and what do we need for that? Enter: Sustainability Indicators, or Targets, or Goals.

Many companies and governments use them.
The European Commission wants Europe to reduce greenhouse gas emissions to at least 55 percent below 1990 levels by 2030.
The Sustainable Development Goals come with lists of targets (#Envision2030).

You can develop your own personal targets and goals. Designers have the advantage that they can visualize and embody this aspirational sustainable future.

At least as important as defining and maintaining indicators is, of course, acting upon them.

The Paris Agreement is a legally binding international treaty on climate change. It was adopted by 196 Parties at COP 21 in Paris, on 12 December 2015. Its goal is to limit global warming to 1.5 degrees Celsius in 2050, compared to pre-industrial levels. The Climate protection index in 2020 revealed that no country is on track.

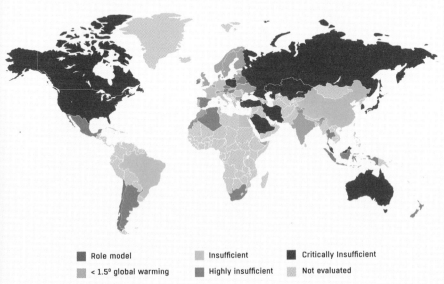

Role model

< 1.5° global warming

Insufficient

Highly insufficient

Critically Insufficient

Not evaluated

TIPS FOR FURTHER READING (in chronological order)

- **United Nations Environment Programme (2009) GUIDELINES FOR SOCIAL LIFE CYCLE ASSESSMENT OF PRODUCTS;** social and socio-economic LCA guidelines complementing environmental LCA and Life Cycle Costing, contributing to the full assessment of goods and services within the context of sustainable development. *unep.org*

- **Serenella Sala, Alessandro Vasta, Lucia Mancini, Jo Dewulf, Eckehard Rosenbaum (2015) SOCIAL LIFE CYCLE ASSESSMENT: State of the art and challenges for supporting product policies.** *Publications Office of the European Union. JRC99101.*

- **Steve Sorrell, Birgitta Gatersleben, Angela Druckman (2017) THE LIMITS OF ENERGY SUFFICIENCY: A review of the evidence for rebound effects and negative spill-overs from behavioural change.** *Energy Research & Social Science. Vol. 64.* Asks the question: can greater use of sufficiency policies and actions help to tackle negative rebounds, or will it create rebounds itself? Spoiler: yes, it will.

- **Rachel Freeman (2018) A THEORY ON THE FUTURE OF THE REBOUND EFFECT IN A RESOURCE-CONSTRAINED WORLD.** *Frontiers in Energy Research Vol. 6.* The study considers four types of rebound effects and explores how the size of these rebound effects might change in future, as supplies of resources from natural capital become more constrained.

- **LIFE CYCLE ASSESSMENT (LCA) – Complete Beginner's Guide.** Online step-by-step guide for making your first LCA. What environmental impact does one object have on the world? *https://ecochain.com/knowledge/life-cycle-assessment-lca-guide/*

- **UNITED NATIONS: ENVISION 2030: 17 goals to transform the world for persons with disabilities.** Website celebrating the inclusion of persons with disabilities in the Sustainable Development Goals. *www.un.org/development/desa/disabilities/envision2030.html*

- **ISO STANDARD 14040: 2006** describes the principles and framework for life cycle assessment. For those ready to take a deep-dive in LCA.

Ryoji Ikeda DATAMATICS (2016)
Datamatics is a series of experiments in various forms – audiovisual concerts, installations, publications, and CD releases – that seek to materialize pure data. In Ikeda's work an effort is made to transform the code which underlies the everyday reality of life into something sublime, simply by enabling us to see and to hear, to understand the language of the data. As Ikeda explains: 'When I set out making this work, my approach was always, first and foremost, that of a composer. Rather than creating a traditional musical composition, I used data as my source material, applying a system and structure as you would with any score.'

10. CELEBRATE

It's quite possible that you can find a counterargument to just about every point made in this book.

Great!

Question everything. Don't blindly follow dogmatic discourse on what should be. Instead, know your own mind and keep it open to what could be.

Where to begin

Projects start with you and your co-workers, a budget, and an objective. Know what you're aiming for.

Establish what the mission is and what the design does. And assess the opposite. Don't overlook what you don't want.

Be pro-active. Assess and extend the influence you have.

Don't underestimate your power. Be a champion of design for sustainability. You'll be surprised at how resistance melts away.

Reframe. Don't try to find the solution, there's no such thing. Stretch the project to incorporate the value of shared sustainability. Twist visions to achieve improvement. Reconsider concepts with all those involved. Inflate financing to include the complete organizational cashflow and prospective investments.

Collaborate, collaborate a lot. Sustainability is huge.

Reach out to experts. It will be a challenge to get them to understand what you need from them, but that's part of your job.

Reach out to amateurs. They understand much more than you think.

Reach out to related businesses. Your interests may merge.

Don't ever forget the people using your products and services – they're crucial. Avoid being naïve about others, their everyday routines and practices, and the way any major sustainability innovation will be resisted. Involve them respectfully when designing.

The Wright brothers designed, built and flew a series of three manned gliders in 1900–1902, marking the beginning of the pioneer era of aviation. Extensive trials of their gliders provided valuable performance data, which was folded back into the evolving design while helping develop piloting skills.

In 'The Museum of Hypothetical Lifetimes' by Mexican artist Pedro Reyes the 'therapist' plays the role of a curator who will help you install a scale version of your life.

How to continue

Take baby steps. Start, for instance, by using recycled plastic in just one component of your product. This may, by the way, be much more difficult than you think. Even such a small step will bring you a wealth of knowledge and new contacts.

Prioritize wisely: If your product is an energy-guzzler, don't focus on recycled plastics; try to find energy efficient solutions instead. When in doubt about priorities, use fast-track life cycle assessment, or ask an expert.

Strategize: Engaging with sustainability concerns the long run. Include the future in your projects and continue to do so. They're never really 'done' and require constant maintenance. Keep an eye out for changing legislation, rebound effects, new technologies and opportunities. Lobby for change, if necessary.

Negotiate: Designing for sustainability is always a negotiation, with possible solutions emerging and dynamically changing over time. Any solution will be fraught with unintended side effects, just like medicines. Think in terms of treatment, like a GP does. Do your level best, monitor, and learn. One step forward, no matter how modest, is a step in the right direction. Celebrate!

At the core of 'Tomorrow is the Question' by the international art collective TeamLab is the issue of our common future.

Grayson Perry's vases are not made for displaying flowers, they are made to softly and critically scream at society.

Authors: Conny Bakker, Ed van Hinte
Graphic design, image editor: Yvo Zijlstra, Antenna-men
English editor: Roger Staats
Made possible with the generous support of TU Delft

BIS Publishers
Borneostraat 80-A
1094 CP Amsterdam
The Netherlands
T +31 (0)20 515 02 30
bis@bispublishers.com
www.bispublishers.com

ISBN 978 90 6369 639 9